Successor journal to *Thea*
VOLUME XVI   PART

FEBRUARY 2000

Editors
CLIVE BARKER
SIMON TRUSSLER

Advisory Editors: Arthur Ballet, Eugenio Barba, Susan Bassnett, Tracy Davis, Martin Esslin, Maggie Gale (*Book Reviews Editor*), Lizbeth Goodman, Peter Hepple, Ian Herbert, Jan Kott, Brian Murphy, Sarah Stanton, Ian Watson

Contents

NICOLAS WHYBROW	3	Animating Morecambe: Forkbeard Fantasy Goes to the Ball *creating a surreal event for a seaside resort which has lost its way*
ELAINE ASTON	17	'Transforming' Women's Lives: Bobby Baker's Performances of 'Daily Life' *the translation of a 'language of food' into live performance*
BARNABY KING	26	Landscapes of Fact and Fiction: Asian Theatre Arts in Britain *Arts Council thinking and the actuality of intra-cultural performance*
GAVIN CARVER	34	The Effervescent Carnival: Performance, Context, and Mediation at Notting Hill *carnival theory and commercial practice in Europe's largest street festival*
DEBORAH SAIVETZ	50	'What Counts is the Landscape': the Making of Pino DiBuduo's 'Invisible Cities' *a decade of 'work in progress' on rediscovering the urban environment*
DEBORAH SAIVETZ	65	'Every Light Form Has a Shadow': Acting in 'Invisible Cities' *how the performers inhabited their 'cities' in the Newark production*
SAM UKALA	76	Impersonation in Some African Ritual and Festival Performance *generic analogies between western 'realism' and African traditions*
DENISE VARNEY AND RACHEL FENSHAM	88	More-and-Less-Than: Liveness, Video Recording, and the Future of Performance *live and mediatized performance, and the need for a theory of 'videocy'*
FRANCES BABBAGE	97	The Past in the Present? A Response to Stan's Cafe's Revival of 'The Carrier Frequency' *myth-making, re-creation, and the problems of documentation*
	100	NTQ Book Reviews *edited by Maggie Gale*

New Theatre Quarterly is published in February, May, August, and November by Cambridge University Press, The Edinburgh Building, Shaftesbury Road, Cambridge CB2 2RU, England   ISBN 0 521 78901 X   ISSN 0266 – 464X

Editorial Enquiries
Oldstairs, Kingsdown, Deal, Kent CT14 8ES, England (e-mail: simon@country-setting.co.uk)

Unsolicited manuscripts are considered for publication in *New Theatre Quarterly*. They should be sent to Simon Trussler at the above address, but unless accompanied by a stamped addressed envelope (UK stamp or international reply coupons) return cannot be guaranteed. Contributors should follow the journal's house style as closely as possible. A style sheet is available on request.

Subscriptions
New Theatre Quarterly (ISSN: 0266-464X) is published quarterly by Cambridge University Press, The Edinburgh Building, Shaftesbury Road, Cambridge CB2 2RU, UK, and The Journals Department, 40 West 20th Street, New York, NY 10011-4211, USA.

Four parts form a volume. The subscription price, which includes postage (excluding VAT), of Volume XVI, 2000, is £55.00 (US$90.00 in the USA, Canada and Mexico) for institutions, £32.00 (US$50.00) for individuals ordering direct from the publishers and certifying that the Journal is for their personal use. Single parts cost £15.00 (US$25.00 in the USA, Canada and Mexico) plus postage. EU subscribers (outside the UK) who are not registered for VAT should add VAT at their country's rate. VAT registered subscribers should provide their VAT registration number. Prices include delivery by air. Japanese prices for institutions are available from Kinokuniya Company Ltd., P.O. Box 55, Chitose, Tokyo 156, Japan.

Orders, which must be accompanied by payment, may be sent to a bookseller or to the publishers (in the USA, Canada and Mexico to the North American Branch). Periodicals postage paid at New York, NY, and at additional mailing offices. POSTMASTER: send address changes in the USA, Canada and Mexico to *New Theatre Quarterly*, Cambridge University Press, The Journals Department, 40 West 20th Street, New York, NY 10011-4211.

Claims for missing issues will only be considered if made immediately on receipt of the following issue.

Information on *New Theatre Quarterly* and all other Cambridge journals can be accessed via http://www.cup.cam.ac.uk/ and in North America via http://www.cup.org/.

Copying: This journal is registered with the Copyright Clearance Center, 222 Rosewood Drive, Danvers, MA 01923. Organizations in the USA who are registered with C.C.C. may therefore copy material (beyond the limits permitted by Sections 107 and 108 of US copyright law) subject to payment to C.C.C. of the per-copy fee of $9.50. This consent does not extend to multiple copying for promotional or commercial purposes. Code 0266-464X/2000 $9.50.

Organizations authorized by the Copyright Licensing Agency may also copy material subject to the usual conditions. ISI Tear Sheet Service, 35021 Market Street, Philadelphia, Pennsylvania 19104, USA, is authorized to supply single copies of separate articles for private use only.

For all other use, permission should be sought from the Cambridge University Press.

© 2000 CAMBRIDGE UNIVERSITY PRESS

The Edinburgh Building, Cambridge CB2 2RU, United Kingdom
40 West 20th Street, New York, NY 10011-4211, USA
10 Stamford Road, Oakleigh, Melbourne 3166, Australia

Typeset by Country Setting, Kingsdown, Deal, Kent CT14 8ES
Printed and bound in the United Kingdom at the University Press, Cambridge

Nicolas Whybrow

Animating Morecambe: Forkbeard Fantasy Goes to the Ball

Forkbeard Fantasy is one of Britain's oldest 'alternative' performance companies. Founded in 1974 by the brothers Tim and Chris Britton, who have continued to work with the company ever since, Forkbeard's practice may be identified with a peculiarly British variant on performance art, which dates from the mid-sixties. Influenced as much by elements of variety entertainment as by early twentieth-century avant-garde movements in the visual arts, it produced a unique form of integrated performance which was often daringly experimental yet refreshingly tongue-in-cheek. In the Spring of 1999, Nicolas Whybrow, then teaching at Lancaster University, observed the company's residency in Morecambe, on the Lancashire coast, over a period of three weeks. Here, he presents his impressions based on a consideration of Morecambe's identity as a place and the nature of Forkbeard's relationship to that place as residential visitors. His analysis takes into account the activities he observed – including his daily trips into Morecambe by train, media 'takes' on the town, informal conversations with contributors to the residency, and a formal interview with the company itself, represented here by interjections into the text. Nicolas Whybrow is now Senior Lecturer at De Montfort University, Leicester.

HEADING NORTH, the near-empty commuter train leaves the West Coast mainline shortly after Lancaster and sweeps broadly shorewards. Before long, Morecambe's flat suburban sprawl sets in as the train slows from a trundle to a roll, virtually floating now between neat rows of grey-pink, pebble-dash bungalows. A spring sun lightly bakes the scene. Greening trees ripple and sway in a gentle seaside breeze. No flutter of a net curtain nor furtive tilt of a venetian blind hints at any sign of human life. My eyelids drooping, I picture myself on David Lynch's fire-engine at the opening of *Blue Velvet* (1986), coasting in soporific slow motion through a small-town neighbourhood somewhere in the American Midwest.

Five minutes later we have drifted into Morecambe Station. Not that you would have noticed. There's a platform on one side, yes, but two-lane traffic on the other, and it's only when you step off and make your way to the top end of this terminus stop that you spy anything like a railway station building. Actually it's more like a glorified bus shelter, a square glass box next to a roundabout with a few metal benches and a single ticket counter, only open till 3 p.m. It's all quite well conditioned, though, because this is the *new* station, opened in 1995.

The *old* station is on the sea front, about half a kilometre away. Follow the road past the Blockbuster Video and Burger King to Morrison's superstore, cross over to Fatty Arbuckle's, turn the corner, and you find yourself on the broad old-station forecourt. Diagonally opposite, precisely on the promenade, lies the dilapidated, art-deco splendour of the Midland Hotel. And right behind that, jutting prominently into the bay, the Stone Jetty where ships from Ireland used to dock. Stretching at least a kilometre either way is the mixed expanse of Morecambe's holiday entertainment and accommodation strip.

Never likely, admittedly, to look its best out of season, the town seems to cower now in the ghostly shadow of its former self. Having long lost out in the amusement-resort stakes to the more imposing Blackpool down the coast, the whole bay area is in fact in the process of readjusting its point of attraction for visitors (and doubtless inhabitants, too) as a natural seabird sanctuary.

Since its location is directly opposite the southern foothills of the Lake District, that appears to make some sense. In the interim, however, a moulting Morecambe struggles with the cultural reality of poverty, abandonment and infrastructural dilapidation. Behind Morrison's superstore, the weeds and shrubs poking wildly through the tracks of the old helter-skelter – the original one, bequeathed to the world by Mr Helter in 1909 – attest to the decline.

Where forms of amusement persist, the scale of risk and ambition is evidently less. Even the harmless cheap thrill promised by the twopenny arcades seems to have synthesized into its opposite: the dismal enshrinement of acute human boredom. Ironically, the visitors Morecambe has now gained the reputation for attracting are Social Security migrants. Settled there from other parts of the country, they are permitted to claim benefit for their occupation of the abundant and obsolete bed and breakfast accommodation on offer. And it is a statistic that the rates of drug abuse and crime are high. But that's just one take on the place.

Some of the poignancy of the creeping transition taking place – whether that be viewed as terminal decline or renewal in waiting – seemed to be captured in the Spring of 1999 in a brief media 'skirmish' involving the local and national press. Both parties appeared to lay claim to conveying the truth about Morecambe with their contrasting portrayals of the place. In the kind of piece which exemplifies the sometimes marginal distinction between tabloid and quality journalism, the London-based *Observer* indulged in a generalized comparison between Morecambe and the west London suburb of Hillingdon, based on the dichotomous quantity of anti-depressants prescribed per head of the populations.[1] Against 'happy Hillingdon', Morecambe emerges as the 'most miserable place in the land', pronounced by one inhabitant as 'gone to the dogs' and by another as 'a filthy town, full of rude people and vandals'.

For the town's weekly newspaper, the *Visitor* this condemnation represented front-page newsworthiness, to say nothing of a counter-attacking editorial feature. Nicely 'fanning the flames of controversy', the *Visitor* countered from a position of 'hurt pride', drawing attention to the previous Bank Holiday weekend, when 'thousands and thousands [of] tourists and locals alike, all looking pretty happy to be here, [were] out and about . . . enjoying the sea air, the views across the bay, and the super new facilities all along the front'.[2]

Ultimately, of course, the underlying motives of both parties are the same – each seeking to project an image of Morecambe that happens to suit its particular selling agenda. Neither is really concerned with the place itself, nor the welfare of the people who live there. Morecambe's problems, its vulnerability, is 'fair game' so far as the media are concerned, whether that be to talk it up or down. Tacitly, then, the apparent opposition here of local versus national might be said to produce 'ideal partners in crime'.

'Placing' Performance Art

In the same month the national journal for practising artists in Britain, *AN Magazine*, ran an article on arts provision in the Lancaster and Morecambe areas. Welcoming recent injections into the region of lottery funding running into millions for various arts projects, it proceeded to highlight what it termed 'a distinct "art" gap when it comes to the interpretation and funding of public art . . . and the actual work produced'.[3] Bewailing the lack of continuous support for artists working in the area in the form of commissions and exhibiting space, the writer poured scorn on the priorities of an award-winning £1.35 million public arts project, part of a long-term regeneration scheme for Morecambe begun in 1995. The centrepiece – unveiled by the Queen – is a statue of the comedian Eric Morecambe, who of course adopted his seaside birthplace as his stage name.

The same article also draws attention to Morecambe's latest arts venue, The Platform, an earlier beneficiary of the regeneration scheme – again, though, lamenting its lack of exhibition space. As its name intimates, The

Exterior of The Platform – the old Morecambe Station, principal point of arrival of holidaying hordes.

Platform is housed in the old promenade railway station, formerly the principal point of arrival of the holidaying hordes. It's an Edwardian sandstone building, opened in 1907, with a wide but deceptively low-slung frontage: a terminus station, featuring above its entrance a roman-numeral clock, with an elegant glass-roof awning supported by stanchions overhanging the immediate forecourt. Inside, the vast, elevated roof above the concourse is also made of glass, producing an atmosphere acutely sensitive to weather changes. It is this space, the size of a sports hall, that has become a performance venue, mainly for concerts.

What Amriding's article does not mention is an initiative by the Nuffield Theatre at Lancaster University – a receiving venue for professional touring theatre – which involves commissioning eight separate and varied practitioners or companies to create a piece of work at the theatre or in residence in the area. The programme, entitled 'Live Wire', will witness a succession of new work emerging over a period of three years.[4] The second company to be commissioned was Forkbeard Fantasy, an internationally renowned group of performance artists based in South-West England which celebrated its twenty-fifth birthday in 1999.

The commission entailed being in residence at The Platform for three weeks in April and May, working with a range of interest groups towards a final production called *Morecambe Dancing*. As the title suggests, this would be based on the format of the popular television show of the 1970s and 1980s, *Come Dancing*, in which modern and old-time sequence dancing couples would compete – rather as in ice-skating – on a regional knock-out basis for a national prize.[5]

Apart from the company itself, the piece would be performed by some twenty-five students engaged in A-level, foundation, or degree work in Performing or Visual Arts at three local colleges[6] – each being required to create a life-size 'ideal dancing partner'. Also involved would be a jazz orchestra based at The Platform, called Off the Rails, and videomakers from Folly Pictures, a Lancaster film production company. Also, two sequence-dancing specialists were to give dance tuition in weekly classes at The Platform. Administrative staff from the venue and from the Live Wire project were asked to take on performing roles as members of the 'judging panel' for the dance competition.

Forkbeard Fantasy's practice belongs to a particular wing of performance art which surfaced in Britain during the 1960s. While now long past the golden age of the following decade, it continues to thrive in small but significant pockets of activity.

The epitome of longevity is doubtless the People Show, which not only emerged as one of the first companies (in 1965) but also took, symbolically, to numbering its productions rather than giving them titles. Wryly recognizing but also celebrating its age and pretensions to eternal life, the company has long since passed its centenary, carrying its bat with *The People Show 107* at the last count.

This style of performance art is a hybrid that is decidedly British, drawing partly on working-class traditions of music hall as well as on the zany humour of *The Goon Show*. The other main source of influence derives from the avant garde – above all surrealist and dadaist experimentation – but, having emerged when it did, it is also frequently marked by a non-aligned political commitment to 'bringing about a better world'. Referring to its roots, Nick Kaye sums it up thus:

British 'performance art' of the late 1960s and early 1970s was not only shadowed by the strength of the politically radical and largely text-based alternative British theatre, but shared some of its practices and concerns. Developing, largely, through work in art or music schools . . . companies such as the People Show, IOU Theatre, and Forkbeard Fantasy drew on the popular entertainments (Henri, 1974) through which many radical political theatres were attempting to define a new working class theatre (McGrath, 1981). . . . These highly visual theatres were characterized by an intuitive rather than systematic play between image, text, and narrative, by inventiveness, and a marked comic eccentricity.[7]

Other recurring features include a preoccupation with technology. This is manifested not in an enthralled embracing of the latest innovations, but rather in a low-tech process of ironic deconstruction – a concern to express fascination on the one hand, whilst throwing the disarming spanner of human ordinariness and fallibility into the works on the other.

There is a clear scientific-age whiff of the eccentric, mad-cap inventor about all this, which seems at once male and remote – what you might call a very boyish kind of obsessiveness – and it is also distinctly British, invoking the modest, loving spirit of do-it-yourself, garden-shed hobbyism. The construction of and performance with kinetic contraptions carries with it a celebration of both humble craftsmanship and street-barking showmanship – the desire to claim some credit and glamour for a humdrum existence in a cut-throat world. The scope this presents for comic absurdity is all too apparent, though it can also carry overtones of nostalgic indulgence in its tendency to hark back to the past.

Animation and the Use of Film

In Forkbeard Fantasy's case, some of these characteristics have been articulated in their recent work through the innovative use of film and life-size 'puppets' or 'dummies', generally operated manually by an 'accompanying character'. Both devices serve in their own ways as screens, simultaneously veiling and reflecting aspects of (other) characters' selves or the situations in which they find themselves.

Tim Britton *They're a form of animation really, aren't they? You do create a living entity through both methods of film and puppetry.*

Chris Britton *The way we interact with film is a bit like using puppets that are us. It's like a mirror or extension.*

Penny Saunders *I've made about six Chrises and slightly fewer Tims. I've made Tims going right down to an inch high. We don't have much of a barrier between our reality and lots of other kinds of reality that we can use in theatre, so film is a reality on a surface, two dimensional. And we don't see animation just in human beings. We can very easily put it somewhere else. You can have a table that's animated, to such an extent that it's got a character and a mission in life.*[8]

Forkbeard Fantasy's favoured filmic technique is to confound audience perceptions of the 'real' and the 'constructed' by having characters walk off stage and, seemingly, on to (pre-recorded) film, or vice versa. Hence characters are seen to intervene or get caught up in filmed action as well as to 'escape' from it, or even to effect its destruction or its distortion in some way. Specifically, the notion of causality is unsettled by this process – as Tim White here analyzes in relation to time:

Though the spatial contiguity of film image and live performer affords much of the humour, the temporal convergence is more disorientating. Undermining the integrity of the past questions the distinctness of the present. Events that unfold on stage cannot be regarded as unequivocally present because they are dependent on what has already passed, whereas this prior moment looks forward to the present for validation.[9]

Generally, the symbolic film 'reel' draws attention to the constructedness of what is taken to be 'real', and emphasizes the degree to which the human subject is entrapped in the 'always already' or 'pre-recordedness' of language.[10]

On the one hand, cleverly 'crossing the celluloid divide' in such a way potentially extends the dimensions of performance, permitting the amusing introduction of outside locations as well as projections of what might be going on immediately behind the scenes. On the other hand, it might be argued that this limits possibilities, in as much as it imposes a singular determining convention whose pattern can quickly become repetitive.

The successful functioning of the device is probably dependent on whether it is brought into play primarily *as* a device or as the main focus of attention – that is, as subject-matter, or even as an animated character in its own right. Thus, its most resonant application has doubtless been in the company's Brittonioni Brothers shows, in which the two film-making siblings, Timmy and Chrissy, show their repertoire of 'fabulous oeuvres'.[11] Taking on the personae of film-makers screening their avant-garde works, in the course of which things begin to go wrong, produces a comic vehicle for the company to suggest 'by accident' the truly innovative possibilities of film beyond simple representation – as White's description suggests:

The work switches direction when, during the projection of *Who Shot the Cameraman?*, an unknown anorak-clad figure makes an appearance in the film. The brothers determine the figure is not 'a hair in the gate' (of the projector) but an intruder who somehow has infiltrated the celluloid since it was shot. To remove the trespasser who is gleefully running around on the film, Chrissy leans behind the screen on which the film is projected. As he does so, his head appears on the screen, even as the audience can see the rest of his body on the stage, crossing 'the celluloid divide'. Once this has been breached, all manner of transactions occur across the space. A priceless camera seen on film is retrieved by Chrissy stepping out of the film into the auditorium, whilst Timmy (on stage) appears to hold a telephone conversation with his brother (on film).[12]

Democracy and Demystification

Above all, perhaps, Forkbeard Fantasy is concerned to demystify the 'silver screen's' false exclusivity and glamour, and to reveal instead both its wondrous sophistication *and* its straightforward accessibility as a medium by expertly applying it in reality in a way that generates apparent chaos and confusion on stage. What the company *presents* is akin to performing the parts of two incompetent magicians, who – precisely through their incompetence – unwittingly reveal the simple secrets and beauty of the art they would seek to master. Thus the audience is given the pleasure not only of seeing the mechanics of film exposed – projectors are usually fully visible on stage – but also of recognizing its potential as a hands-on, experimental phenomenon.

Penny Saunders *I'd love it if we could demystify the film industry so that people could sit and watch a film and say, 'Oh, it's just a film, that's just Robert Redford.' Because it's got so bent now. People have become so obsessed with fame and so taken in by the film industry – I mean subliminally – it's dangerous. I don't think they remember sometimes where the line is between their own lives and what they get through films. I always hope through having the film on stage and walking in and out of it, we're kind of reducing its power a bit.*

Tim Britton *And rediscovering it as an art form, because when it was invented it had a* *completely different use. It took a completely different shape and form to what it became. It only became a kind of narrative form round about the 1920s, and then every single film that was made started to have a bloody story, and a beginning, middle, and end – and titles, and 'The End' at the end, and the credits. Yet the earliest experimenters in film were magicians. They were playing with it as an illusion, as a fantastic magic trick, which of course it was. One of the first showings was a train coming towards the audience and everyone leapt up and ran out of the cinema. They used to just sit and watch a static shot of cars driving past on an empty street or people walking past.*[13]

The ironic, anti-illusionistic action of Forkbeard Fantasy's approach produces part of what might be referred to as a democratizing aesthetic. High technology – the god that is the film industry – is subverted by low-tech antics which call into question our seduction by idealized protagonists repeatedly playing out triumphs over evil others.

Anti-heroes like the Brittonioni Brothers aspire to be part of all the glitz, but it is when their distinct *lack* of glamour emerges that they endear themselves to us as the fallible mortals they really are. Whilst their blundering delusions makes us glad we are *not* like them, they have served to show us the shortcomings of the pretentious world of film production.

A significant part of Forkbeard's craft lies in the tension created by visibly running the risk of failure or disaster in its shows.[14] It is evident to an audience that there is a high reliance on technology working properly. In its most recent piece, *The Barbers of Surreal* (1999), for example, five separate projectors showing pre-recorded material were used. The importance of timing, both in cuing-in films – which the actors do on stage – and of interacting with them correctly as live actors is paramount.[15] Added to that is the challenge of making everything *appear* to be out of control.

In other words, everything *functions* to produce *mal*functioning. Hence, the *threat* of disaster is one that has both a planned dimension, as a comic effect, and an unplanned one – a possible missed cue or a faulty projector. And such mishaps do occur, which the performers use all their improvisational wiles to rectify – because, on principle, a show is never halted.

Tim Britton *The films do go wrong, lots of things do, and you just keep going. Well, you change course slightly and then try and get back on track again.*

Ed Jobling *That's where it would tip into* real *chaos, but it doesn't because you have got that sense of order behind it, so you know what you've got to do to get back to the order when things go wrong. So, if the projector doesn't work for some reason, you've got back-up. It can never just fold on us.*[16]

Naturally, performing chaos as well as running the real risk of it occurring on account of the technical complexity involved – the latter being as much part of the aesthetic as the former – presupposes a high degree of discreet control and discipline. It is precisely that contrast which lends credibility to the company's desire to subvert the myth of high-tech opulence and exclusivity. Performing such improbable acts requires guile. The trick is expertly to pull off the stunt as a performer when the odds seem to be stacked against you as a character.

'Dis-placing': Morecambe Dancing

There is a way in which things come in twos with Forkbeard Fantasy. I have talked about the conjunction of order and chaos, the film screen as veil and reflector – even, as White suggests, window and barrier[17] – and the interaction of the 'real' and 'reel', live and pre-recorded, present and past. Much of the company's practice, moreover, is predicated on a double-act format, one which clearly seeks to play on the link between performers and stage personae: the Britton brothers on the one hand, the Brittonionis on the other. Even the company's name carries connotations of duality: the alliteration, the image of a two-pronged beard.

But it is important to recognize that these couplings are complementary rather than

The setting for the final event, the performance of *Morecambe Dancing*.

binary opposites – part of a continuum, in which two entities 'produce' one another, as opposed to either being privileged. To expound on this further I will concentrate presently on Forkbeard's specific use of life-size, animated puppets or dancing partners. First, though, I will set the scene of its residency and the performance event in which it culminated.

Penny Saunders *What a strange place The Platform is, because although it's not a station any more, people still seem to come and go.*[18]

Forkbeard Fantasy spent three weeks in residence at The Platform in Morecambe. Although well acquainted with the practice of producing work in 'strange places' with 'co-opted' groups of people, the company does not view itself as specifically interested in 'site' or 'location' as points of departure. Generally speaking, it is more concerned simply to introduce its working methods – less according to the principle of 'passing on genius' than to generate a flurry of creative activity within the imposed framework of the company's particular aesthetic.

Whilst this sort of approach certainly applied in the case of Morecambe, there was also a precise way – as the title of the piece implies – in which the location *did* figure significantly. Not only did Forkbeard see an opportunity to integrate a popular local form of recreation – sequence or tea dances – within the parodied format of a well-known television show, it was also conscious of staging an event for a specific *spectating* as well as participating constituency of people from the area. So the title *Morecambe Dancing*, as well as implying that the piece was *about* the place, also contained an invitation.

Forkbeard Fantasy's residency signified a form of negotiation of some distinct temporal and/or spatial states. While acknowledging Morecambe the place as a continuous phenomenon with a particular identity, the company also sought to engineer a provisional place-within-a-place – a temporary *dis*placement – in the form of events leading to an event. In this sense, The Platform, as the continuing embodiment of '*constant* coming and going', served as a symbolic point of convergence, if not conflation, of temporal and spatial conditions: a permanent architectural fixture whose function is to facilitate transience.

Tripping the Light Fantastic

The final event itself, a one-off performance, attracted a capacity audience. Making use of the entire ex-station concourse, Forkbeard designated the central section of the venue as the performing area, with the audience sitting round tables on either side. A raised stage accommodated the jazz orchestra and the two comperes of the event – the Britton brothers – with the panel of judges immediately opposite and a large ballroom-space in between.

The show begins, and the two comperes – improvising wildly and relying entirely on the sheer 'excess' of their characters, Chris cross-dressed and Tim as a sleazy entrepreneur – proceed to introduce staggered groupings of dancing couples, who make grand entrances before turning a number round the floor. Directly prior to a grouping's introduction, the audience is shown a pre-recorded video clip of the waiting couples, staged as if it were occurring live in the dressing rooms. Thus, Forkbeard's customary trick of 'crossing the celluloid divide' is incorporated – while the sequences also parody the bland biographical inserts employed in *Come Dancing* by pointing to various backstage dramas going on, which are reminiscent of Baz Luhrmann's film *Strictly Ballroom* (1992). For example, there are malicious attempts to sabotage the competition.

Once all the pairs have completed their dances and the judges have delivered their farcical verdicts, all the puppets are left dangling from elasticated ropes in the dance space. An interval is declared, in which the audience is invited to replenish its drinks and to 'get acquainted' with the bobbing puppets. The second half of the evening then turns into a dance party, with the jazz band churning out numbers, and with anyone who desires choosing their 'ideal partner' with whom to 'trip the light fantastic'.

Judged purely as a performance, the event contained many rough edges. Thus, the connection between filmed sequences, dancing, and judging was tenuous and ultimately inconsequential, while the two comperes struggled to maintain an effective performance tension. It was probably difficult for a complete outsider to make proper sense of what was being performed.

However, it is important to put this in perspective. In the first place, Forkbeard Fantasy regarded the event more as a 'showing' than a full-scale performance. In this respect the event functioned effectively as a vehicle for displaying the work of the residency, similar to a fashion show or cat-walk parade. Second, the ramshackle nature of the event in fact corresponded closely to the company's characteristic courting of incompetence. Hence, the flirtation with the possibility of it '*not* being all right on the night' was at least to some degree an intended feature of the performance, as well as one to hide behind.

Finally, and despite those reservations regarding the outsider's view, the event as a whole provoked a rousing atmosphere of enthusiastic involvement on the part of the spectators as well as performers. It is always difficult to gauge the precise make-up of an audience. Aside from being able readily to identify a considerable generational mix in this case, it *seemed* at least that the majority consisted of friends and relatives of performing participants, accounting not only for voluble support at times during the performance – as if it were a sporting contest – but great subsequent interest in the puppets, and uninhibited involvement in the dancing.

The Aesthetics of Democratization

The performances overall thus produced an extended community of participants who would not normally have attended such an occasion. The aggregate response clearly embraced the invitation proffered by the title of the event – effecting, then, a significant transference in the process of animation from the

Top: the jazz orchestra. Bottom: 'choosing an ideal partner' to dance the light fantastic.

bodies of the performing puppets and their chaperones to the collective body politic.

For the participating performers, most of the time had been spent making a 'dance partner' in the main Platform space. Working from initial designs and supervised by members of Forkbeard, they used materials such as plastic plumbing pipes and ping-pong balls to make bones and joints, bubble wrap and insulation foam to flesh-out the bodies, and muslin for skin to construct the 'ideal' body of a life-size partner.

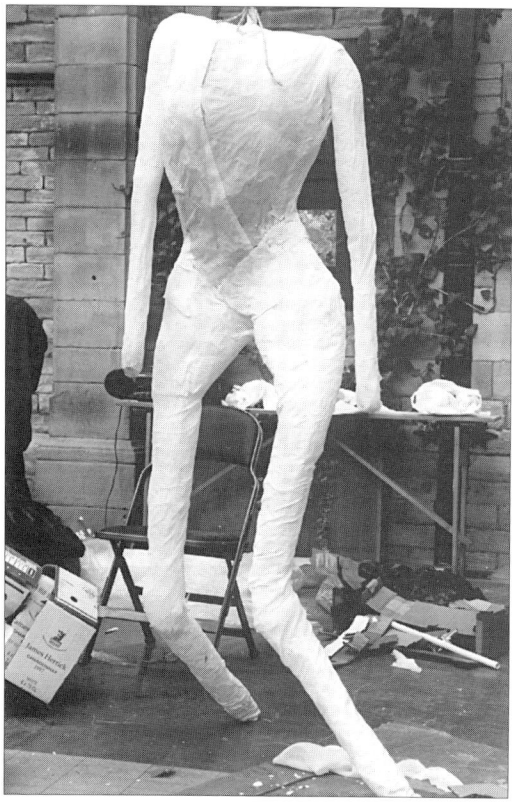

Penny Saunders *One thing we hope people who participate in our residencies get out of them is an incredible availability of materials, which is a real luxury that a lot of people don't usually have. And we spend a lot on materials. Then there's also the expertise and experience that we've had, which enables them to achieve something quicker than if they were trying to find out by themselves. The big thing is a political one, though: the more people who understand and enjoy art, the better world we're going to live in.*[19]

Forkbeard Fantasy is a *making* company. It has thus emerged from the world of visual art rather than theatre, and the process of personally constructing every detail of the performance environment for any piece is central to an understanding of its practice. Each member of the company possesses a favoured emphasis – whether that be making animated puppets or shooting films – but all are to some degree involved in every aspect.

The notion of 'making what you perform with(in)', of having handled the materials, contributes to a powerful sense of an integrated aesthetic in performance. It is what enables elaborate multimedia trickery not only to be employed but also to work – or to be 'corrected', as an effective part of the performance, if it does go off the rails. It also represents a further dimension of the company's democratizing ethos, conveying as it does a strong feeling of shared ownership of the work.

This feature of Forkbeard's practice takes on a particular significance, perhaps, when applied to its residential work. Participants are similarly *given responsibility* for performing with what they have been making, an opportunity which naturally implies wielding the double-edged sword of being able to 'show off', on the one hand, whilst flirting with the risk of failure on the other. Hence, central pillars of the company's performance aesthetic – including demystifying the 'high gloss' or 'unattainability' of the art-making process – transfer seamlessly into the workshop methodology, pointing up the way Forkbeard does effectively become an 'extended company' in such situations.[20]

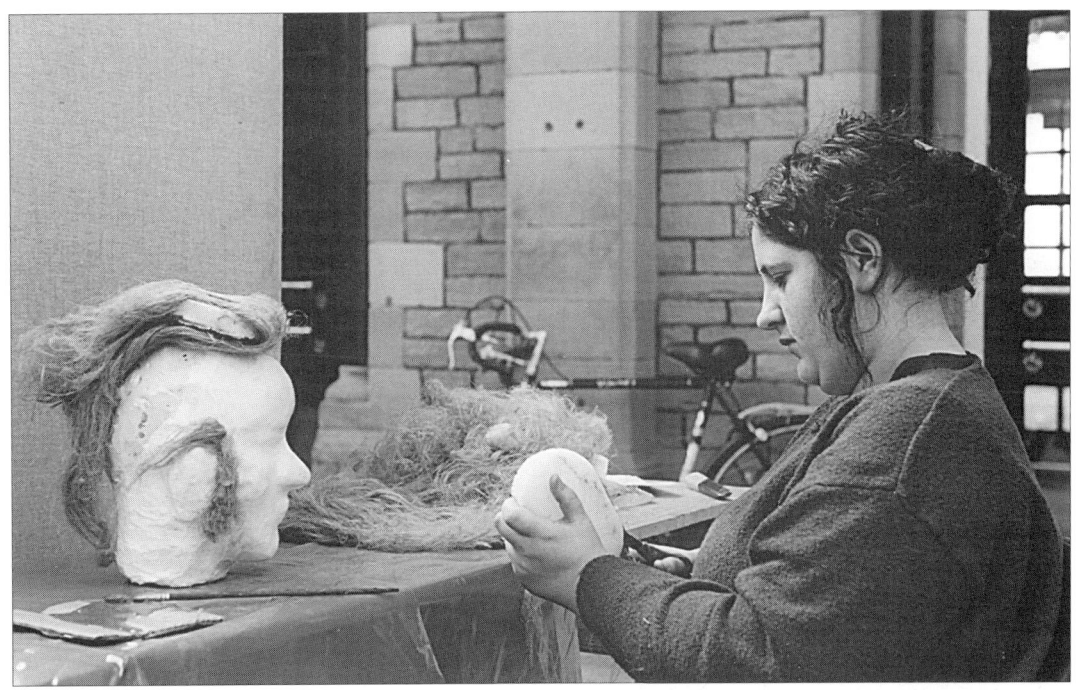

Ideal Partners

The attention to detail of the working process was meticulous, requiring from the beginning a clear sense of how the performer wished the puppet to move as well as how he or she wished to move with *it*. Hence, a form of dual interrogation took place, which incorporated both anatomy and kinaesthesis: 'How are we structured?' and 'How do we work?' as well as 'How do we move?' – or, perhaps more accurately, 'How do we move in tandem?'

So: what is an ideal partner? The brief given by Forkbeard inevitably produced a wide range of generic responses, ranging from the two-dimensionality of an 'Elvis figure' or a 'sad anorak' character to the more abstract 'Eggman' and 'Buddha', as illustrated overleaf. It was not just a matter of inventing a partner, though, since the makers themselves also adopted personae. In effect, they were creating a performing pair of which they acted both halves simultaneously. In *this* sense the degree of abstraction or two-dimensionality (or *whatever*) was irrelevant, since the significance lay in the interrelationship of the character construct as embodied (or operated) by a

Opposite page and above: 'dancing partners' in various stages of construction.

Below: getting 'a clear sense of how the performer wished the puppet to move'.

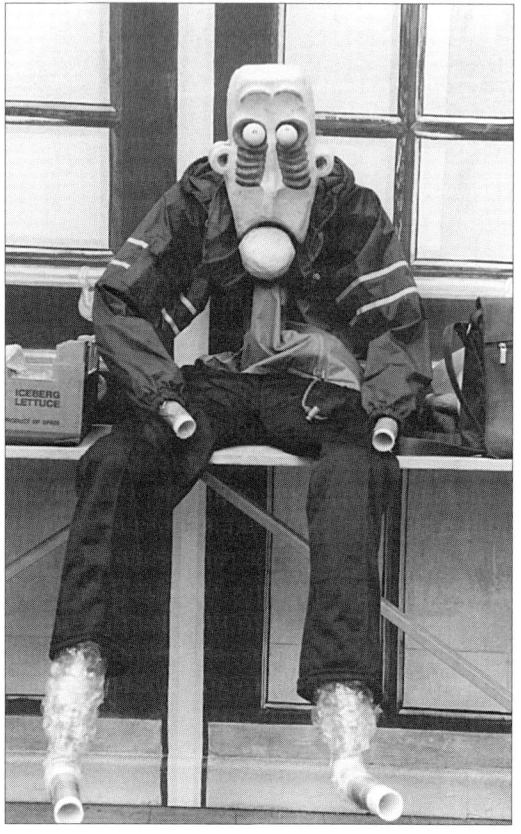

single performer, rather than between the real person (or manipulator) and his or her fictive 'other'.

As with the personae of the Brittonioni Brothers and their interaction with film, a framework is here established within which to interrogate the complex slippage between the reflection and projection or mirror and screen. However, the framework here corresponds to a form of distanciated staging of a veiling – not unlike adopting a Janus-faced mask – in which the performer remains visible as also manipulator. As with film, the company both uses the trickery of the device *and* reveals it for what it is. It functions in effect as a performed paradigm of (self)-see(k)ing, or more accurately the distortion contained in that process.

The performer projects into the partnership in an attempt to play out or discover (have reflected back) something about him/herself, whilst simultaneously remaining outside it, becoming, as it were, a spectator to his/her own performance. In so doing, the performer is inevitably faced with the contradiction, universally posed for the subject, of being required to seek the self in the other(s) – as Peggy Phelan explains:

Identity is perceptible only through a relation to an other – which is to say, it is a form of both resisting and claiming the other, declaring the boundary where the self diverges from and merges with the other. In that declaration of identity and identification, there is always loss, the loss of not-being the other and yet remaining dependent on that other for self-seeing, self-being....

In looking at the other (animate or inanimate) the subject seeks to see itself. Seeing is an exchange of gazes between a mirror (the image seen which reflects the looker looking) and a screen (the laws of the symbolic which define subject and object positions within language). Looking, then, both obscures and reveals the looker.[21]

Phelan's observation can also be linked to the way the paradigm in question does not amount so much to an opposition as a continuum (as I have suggested earlier), in which the subject's identity is not established by the exclusion, suppression, or exploitation of the other, but by admitting dependence on it, a process which highlights

Opposite page, top: a 'sad anorak character'. Opposite page, bottom: 'a performing pair', acting both halves simultaneously. Above: masks for Eggman and Buddha. All photos in this feature by courtesy of the author.

their mutually constructed states of being. Significantly, the operation of this mechanism occurs physically through conjoined bodies in movement. Emphasizing the body in this way, as the site of contested identity, marks, in Lacanian terms,[22] an understanding of the biological condition as symbolically interpreted, of culture as imposing meaning on anatomical parts. Thus, the preoccupation with anatomy in the process of constructing the animated puppets was predicated on a 'known grammar of movement'. To invoke Phelan again briefly: the 'given-to-be-seen *belongs* to the field of knowledge of the one who looks' – or, in this case, *makes*.[23]

This is portrayed as an organic process of development – from bones to joints, to skeletal configurations, to flesh and skin, and so on – culminating in a form of prosthetic doubling. Invariably an artificial extension of the body such as this is seen as limited in its efficiency, as fallible. Its deficiencies of expression in movement – indicative of its entry into the symbolic order – are precisely what determine its 'personality'. In this way it functions to perform both the constructed nature of identity and the lacking 'wholeness' which that inevitably implies. Thus, we learn that the organism is always incomplete or constrained in some way in its state of being encoded.

In general terms, Forkbeard Fantasy's practice plays on the interface of the mechanical and the 'human'. But whereas experimental practitioners like Stelarc and the Wooster Group – who can be said to entertain related areas of concern – embrace the 'inevitability of progress', preoccupied as they are with the post-organic performer or with the notion of re-naturalizing, through technology, the obsolescent human body precisely on account of its 'failings', Forkbeard's inclination is to continue to celebrate the imperfect but nevertheless 'organic' human being. Hence, with ironic amusement, the company concentrates on the surreal quirks and absurdities which 'life' in an alienating modern world produces, and continuously seeks to recover the 'human being' or 'humanity' from its constraining clutches.

Ultimately Forkbeard Fantasy is interested in what might bring people together – in animating the body politic – rather than what divides individuals from themselves. So, whereas its practice clearly recognizes the instability and fragmentation of identity as produced by a technological world, its instinct is not to agonize dispassionately, as it were, over such a state of affairs but to channel, or *displace*, that perception into a form of collective 'commiseration' which emerges as the idealized celebration or ritualization of what is perceived to be a commonly held humanity.

Notes and References

1. Richard Thomas, 'Suburban Bliss, Seaside Hell', *The Observer*, 2 May 1999, p. 15.
2. Ingrid Kent, 'Miserable Morecambe?', *Visitor*, 5 May 1999, p. 1; and Town Crier, 'Wrong Image from a Casual Observer', ibid., p. 8.
3. Chris Amriding, 'Visual Art at Bay', *AN Magazine*, May 1999, p. 5.
4. The Live Wire project is funded to the tune of £239,560 over three years from a combination of A4E lottery money (the majority), matched by smaller amounts from city and county council departments and box-office income. The project began in September 1998 with the Nigel Charnock Company in residence at the Nuffield Theatre, Lancaster University, and has been followed by visits from IOU and Russell Maliphant.
5. Competitive dance sequences would be intercut with biographical detail and interviews with couples.
6. The colleges involved were the University College of St. Martin's; Lancaster and Morecambe College; and Morecambe High School.
7. Nick Kaye, 'Live Art: Definition and Documentation', *Contemporary Theatre Review*, II, No. 2 (1994), p. 2. The internal references are respectively to Adrian Henri, *Total Art: Environments, Happenings, and Performance* (New York; Toronto: Oxford University Press, 1974); and John McGrath, *A Good Night Out: Popular Theatre: Audience, Class, and Form* (London: Methuen, 1981).
8. Taped interview, 11 May 1999.
9. Tim White, 'The Screen: Looking through it, Walking through it', *Contemporary Theatre Review*, II, No. 2 (1994), p. 112.
10. This relates, of course, to another 'reel', namely the child's one of the Freudian *fort/da*: see Sigmund Freud, *Beyond the Pleasure Principle*, Standard Edition, XVIII (London: Hogarth Press, 1955). Madan Sarup offers a succinct summary: 'The child had a cotton reel with a piece of string tied to it. Holding the string he would throw the reel over the edge of his cot and utter sounds that Freud interpreted as being an attempt at the German *fort*, meaning "gone" or "away". He would then pull the reel back into his field of vision, greeting its reappearance with a joyful *da* ("there"). This game allowed the eighteen-month-old child to bear without protest the painful experience of his mother's absence, to cope with her disappearance and reappearance. It illustrates the birth of language in its autonomy from reality and allows a better understanding of how language distances us from the lived experience of the real. The distancing is effected in two stages: the child moves from the mother to the reel and finally to language.' As Sarup goes on to point out, Lacan 'interprets the story as being more about the disappearance of the self than that of the mother'. Both, however, see *fort/da* 'as an allegory about the linguistic mastery of the drives'. Hence, the reel, as the first most basic indication of narrative, epitomizes the process by which the human subject becomes codified. See Sarup, *Poststructuralism and Postmodernism* (Hemel Hempstead: Harvester Wheatsheaf, 1993), p. 8, 23.
11. Forkbeard Fantasy, *Forkbeard Theatre and Film Productions: Part 2, 1988–1992* (Devon: Forkbeard Fantasy, 1993).
12. White, op. cit., p. 111.
13. Whybrow, op. cit.
14. Baz Kershaw makes a similar point in relation to Welfare State International in *Engineers of the Imagination: the Welfare State Handbook* (London: Methuen, 1990), p. 218.
15. That does not, of course, take into account the enormous task of pre-planning material before it is filmed – that is, working out exactly what to film and how, so that it interacts appropriately with the live elements.
16. Whybrow, op. cit.
17. White, op. cit., p.113.
18. Whybrow, op. cit.
19. Ibid.
20. The transposition of the aesthetic which takes place here would seem to contain an important lesson, too, for arts funders in their perennial attempts to assess the merits of practice on the basis of 'quality' – or 'excellence'. In this instance, the quality of the practice clearly lies not merely within the confines of Forkbeard's performance aesthetic but also in the *manner of the relationship* it takes to its audience.
21. Peggy Phelan, *Unmarked: the Politics of Performance* (London; New York: Routledge, 1993), p. 13, 16.
22. See Jacques Lacan, trans. Alan Sheridan, *Ecrits: a Selection* (London: Tavistock, 1977).
23. Phelan, op. cit., p. 160.

Elaine Aston

'Transforming' Women's Lives: Bobby Baker's Performances of 'Daily Life'

In an earlier issue of *New Theatre Quarterly*, NTQ55 (August 1998), Marcia Blumberg examined the setting of the kitchen in performances by Bobby Baker and Jeanne Goosen, arguing for the 'transitional and transgressive' possibilities of this domestic-cum-performance space. Here, Elaine Aston returns to the 'kitchen' in Bobby Baker's performances of 'daily life'. The article examines Baker's 'language' of food which 'speaks' of domesticity, and her conjunction of comic playing and the hysterical marking of the body, to show how her performance work constitutes an angry, feminist protest at the lack of social transformation in women's lives. Elaine Aston has authored a number of studies on contemporary women's theatre, and is Chair of Contemporary Performance and Theatre Studies, Lancaster University.

IN THE 1960s, before second-wave feminism, sociology lecturer Hannah Gavron researched the lives of young mothers from middle-class and working-class families in North London. Her research was published posthumously as *The Captive Wife* (1966).[1] Her sub-title, *Conflicts of Housebound Mothers*, points to a domestic and maternal narrative of isolation, frustration, and confinement for women that second-wave feminism began to address and to challenge in the 1970s.

Among the four demands of the liberation movement, the request for twenty-four hour nurseries and free contraception and abortion on demand were central to the possibility of a social metamorphosis of women's maternal and reproductive lives. Despite these feminist demands, however, relatively little was to change. In particular, the conflict for women between the roles of mother and worker, which Gavron had highlighted,[2] if anything grew more acute in the Thatcherite 1980s, which promoted the myth of the Superwoman – the working mother who could 'successfully' combine professional life with family life.

It is hardly surprising, therefore, that Gavron's study remains ominously familiar, and that, despite certain class differences, middle- and working-class mothers with care of young children remain 'isolated from the mainstream of society',[3] and still experience the difficulty of combining work and family.

Performance artist Bobby Baker takes the 'conflicts of housebound mothers' and wives as a key (although not exclusive) subject for her shows. Like the women researched by Gavron in her study, Baker is also a North London mother. She introduces herself – in interviews and in the opening to her shows – as a middle-class housewife and mother of two from London N7. In particular, she marks the tension between motherhood and work. This tension was one which Baker experienced in her own career: after training as an artist, her emergent performance career in the 1970s was interrupted by an eight-year break in which she birthed and cared for her two children. When Baker returned to performance in the late 1980s she created *Drawing on a Mother's Experience*, and in the 1990s established her 'Daily Life' series, which so far includes *Kitchen Show* (1991), *How to Shop* (1993), *Take a Peek!* (1995), and *Grown-Up School* (1999).[4]

That Baker's work imports her autobiographical 'daily life' experiences into a performance context is important. Of course, when the autobiographical 'I' enters the fictional frame of performance it raises many complex questions and issues around identity, authenticity and construction of self – questions which have received consideration elsewhere.[5] What is important in Baker's case is that her observational style of comedy is dependent upon the sense that she has direct experience of the events she describes. As one reviewer explained in a commentary on her 1980 show, *My Cooking Competes*: 'The audience knew that this presenter had actually performed all these tasks, that they had taken up her time, just as they wear away the time of countless women, day after day.'[6]

In this way Baker, like Gavron with her empirically researched mothers, finds a means of introducing the 'real mother' into a sphere of representation from which she is traditionally absent. For instance, in *Motherhood and Representation*, E. Ann Kaplan examines the discursive levels of the socially constructed mother (historical) and the mother in the unconscious (psychoanalytic) in literary and film texts (fictional), but claims that the fourth mother, the 'real life' mother, is not representable.[7] Instead, she hopes that her analysis of historical, psychoanalytic, and fictional mothers will be of some benefit to the 'conflicted, difficult, and marginalized life' of the 'real mother'.

By contrast, it is precisely this 'conflicted, difficult, and marginalized life' of the real mother which Baker introduces by taking herself as subject of and agent for her work. She uses her personal memories, experiences, feelings of her 'real life', or 'daily life' as a middle-aged housewife and mother of two to challenge the socially constructed (historical) role of the mother. Her experiences as a mother combine with her skills as an artist to transform the patriarchally constructed mother by unleashing the intense pains and pleasures conventionally repressed and constrained by this dominant ideological formation.

'Drawing on a Mother's Experience'

Fundamental to Baker's performances of 'daily life' is the way in which she communicates her experiences through the 'language' of food.[8] After formally training as a painter, Baker began to work not with the paints of the artist's palette, but with the colours and textures of the oral palette – of food. Before she began work on food sculpture, she 'among other things . . . danced with meringue ladies, recreated the history of modern painting in sugar, and made a life-size cake family in a sugar-decorated prefab entitled *An Edible Family in a Mobile Home*.[9] Even when her work began to incorporate dialogue, food remained her primary 'language' – a means of communicating the experiences of domestic, 'daily life' which she shared with women in her audiences.[10]

After her eight years away from the stage to have children, Baker returned to performing with her food-painting show, *Drawing on a Mother's Experience*, in which she describes the experiences of becoming a mother and her subsequent transformation into a working mother. In *The Captive Wife* Gavron quotes from a Marriage Guidance Council booklet published in 1963 to describe the time with young children as 'a time of "pots and nappies, crying, feeding and the all important business of burping. It is the most extraordinary mixture of the sublime and the ridiculous, the anxious and the funny".'[11] One might be forgiven for thinking this was a reviewer commenting on *Drawing on a Mother's Experience*.

The performance of *Drawing* begins with Baker laying out a polythene sheet to protect the floor. Onto the polythene she spreads, as neatly as possible, a white double bed-sheet (her 'canvas'), onto which she proceeds to mark the experiences of becoming a mother. Starting in one corner, Baker presses down slices of cold roast beef to make a 'sensitive' mark recalling the birth of her first child. In the style of a Jackson Pollock action painting she makes further marks/memories out of milk, fish pies, stout, yoghurt, blackcurrants, preserves, tea, biscuits, black treacle, egg yokes, and whites. Verbally she refers to herself as a mother who is skilled at thrifty shopping, at recycling materials to avoid waste, and as someone who is most experienced in cleaning and clearing up after others.

Conscious that such daily realities are treated as mundane, boring, and insignificant, she looks for short cuts in her maternal and domestic re-enactments to spare her audience the monotony of time-consuming, labour-intensive tasks, or the embarrassment of the abject, reproductive body. At the close, she exits as she entered – with all her foodstuffs packed into two plastic shopping bags, leaving not a trace of her presence in the performance space.

In *Drawing*, the food painting 'speaks' the anxieties provoked by the idea of the 'successful' mother which women frequently internalize. Many of these are linked to the business of feeding. Baker, for example, narrates the experience of being 'consumed by the worry of feeding', and marks the early days of breast feeding her first child with possets and dribbles of milk on the sheet. But this marks not only her 'success' at being able to breast feed (which she tells us she was able to do to excess), but also the consumption of her own body. As Rosalind Coward explains:

Around the child's feeding, a whole drama is played out around anxiety, around which the adequacy of mothering can be assessed. And this anxiety, produced by medical and scientific opinion, overlays the already anxious relations which a mother and child will have on the subject of food. Such opinion crosses over the unconscious conflicts which a woman experiences between the command to provide, to give out and nourish, and the fear that, in so doing, she may be consumed and disappear altogether.[12]

As Baker's narrative/painting unfolds, her nourishment of the baby raises the issue of who, in turn, will feed the mother. It is possible to read this both literally in terms of the incredible appetite which accompanies breast feeding, and metaphorically – as women's hunger for keeping something of their own lives, their autonomy.

Baker's need for self-nourishment is signed through the action of the stout, bottles of which she rolls across the sheet to produce marks which are more pronounced than the 'sensitive' marks made by the roast beef. She then repeats the action until she succeeds in making the bottles chink – a sound which reminds her of the chink which the empty bottles made as they rattled in the

Bobby Baker in *Drawing on a Mother's Experience*.

pram tray as she bumped her way over the pavement to take the empties back to the off-licence. (Delightfully, she tells us of the troubled gaze of the health visitor who, on one occasion, happened to witness this not-quite-so-'proper' image of the mother.)

The 'Old' Mother and the 'New'

'Drawing on a mother's experience' takes on another or double meaning, as it refers also to Baker's own mother. While the husband is busy rushing off to work, it is Baker's mother, she tells us, who feeds the hungry daughter. Although psychoanlytically the time of becoming a mother is seen as a moment of potential reconciliation between mother and daughter, in reality it may also be a period of difficult and complex negotiation between the 'old' mother and the 'new'; between the different, generational, internalized systems of 'successful' mothering, or between the desire to be a mother and the fear of becoming one's own mother, etc.[13]

Baker gives 'voice' to these generational tensions through the mark of the fish pie: the food her mother brought to nourish her, which had orange crumbs, rather than her own pie with wholemeal crumbs. Then the hidden tensions of drawing on one's own mother's experiences are further imaged in a mark made by a pudding of yoghurt and blackcurrants. On the one hand, this signifies a comforting moment of self-infantilization, with Baker the 'child' who eats up all her mother's puddings, even though she does not like them.[14] On the other hand, the repressed resentment which this occasions explodes in the urge to pop the blackcurrants, to crush them underfoot, and to admire the chroma this produces in the painting: an intensity of pink as the red of the currants dominates the white, milky yoghurt beginnings of the mark.

The lighter colours in the first part of the painting, the early days of mothering, are gradually overlaid by darker colours produced by foodstuffs which, for example, narrate a stressful time of money worries – marked by the strong-smelling, brilliant red of her home-made, money-saving preserves. The birth of a second child, marked by tea, barely makes an impression, and if anything is 'slightly dull' and immediately swamped by strong swirls of black treacle. The treacle hints at a life outside of children as Baker makes reference to her training as a painter and leads into her penultimate sequence: the transformation into a working mother.

Baker chooses to celebrate this transformation with a recipe for a pudding which she recollects making at this time for dinner parties. Preparing food for the entertainment of others is a different kind of cooking ritual: a social occasion, signifying the mother's return to a public life – or rather a working life that she has to combine with the work of mothering. Separating the yokes from the white of the eggs, Baker rushes around the sides of her sheet, trying not to trip up, to attend separately to the preparation of each part of the egg, and, finally, to fold these both into the painting.

The recipe fails if the yoke and the white do not separate – which speaks volumes to those of us whose daily lives are a constant battle to make a life split between children and work more manageable. Very briefly, she takes delight in the feathering effect which this produces before, dramatically, cancelling out her drawing by sifting flour over the whole sheet. There is, she explains, an element which is too painful to talk about. As Griselda Pollock argues: 'The painful memories will not be left, sanitized by their aesthetic look, assimilated back to the action painting they cleverly resemble.'[15]

The white blanket of flour cannot, however, cover up all these marks/memories. Nor should they, as Baker's final sequence suggests, be completely repressed. Instead, Baker rolls herself up in the sheet so as to resemble a 'human swiss roll' and takes these marks on to her body. The struggle to get to her feet, whilst swathed in the marks of maternity, is considerable. She tells us she used to worry she would not get out, but that she learnt not to panic. Then, in a quiet moment of celebration, she begins to dance. Previously she had told us she was not skilled at dancing, but this is a moment in which she pleasures herself – a final *gestus* showing the struggle of the professional artist, successfully emergent from the 'sheet'/ maternal, despite the way in which the body is weighed down, making it difficult to move. Baker's choice of song to dance to, Nina Simone's 'My Baby Just Cares for Me', is, she informs us, not significant: a final ironizing of the mother, who, in truth, is always at risk of being consumed by the act of caring for others.

'Kitchen Show'

While I was researching this article I kept remembering an independent feminist film from the late 1970s which I used to teach for the Open University: *Often During the Day*, directed by Joanna Davis. The film shows several shots of a kitchen, interspersed with extracts of text from Ann Oakley's *The Sociology of Housework* – the text of which is presented both on screen and as voice-over –

and uses a looped sound-track of everyday kitchen noises: tea-pouring, bread-cutting, chairs scraping. The technique of the sound loop effectively brings home the unchanging, mindless, repetitive, endless, and thankless tasks of domesticity. In the film, it is a woman who is imaged as repeatedly clearing up after others. It made for extremely uncomfortable viewing – but that of course was the point .

Like *Often During the Day*, Baker takes the kitchen as her setting for the first in her 'Daily Life' series, *Kitchen Show*. When she began performing *Kitchen Show* in 1991, Baker reinforced the point about the spheres of domesticity/private and work/public by staging the show in her own North London pine kitchen, rather than in a theatre.[16] The piece is structured through twelve daily actions which take place in her kitchen, each of which she marks on her white overalls which have now become a hallmark of her shows.[17]

As she performs each one we hear about the domestic story, event, feeling, experience, sensation, or memory associated with it, delivered in a documentary-style ('to-be-taken-seriously') voice-over. The reviewer for *Time-Out* explains:

Bobby Baker in *Kitchen Show*, as performed at the London International Festival of Theatre, 1991. Photo: Andrew Whittuck

The kitchen is the stage where she presents her private self through twelve actions she might carry out any day, from clearing out the cutlery drawer to rinsing spinach. These are strung together with female confidences, reminiscences, and send-ups of the apologetically appreciative middle-class wife and mother, and her inspired ramblings take the lid off a woman's mind and make sense and nonsense of the routines of running a home.[18]

Baker re-presents the kitchen as a site of many mixed emotions and pleasures: of anger (marked by the action of hurling a pear to relieve tension); of joy (as she rinses and peels carrots under running tap water); or of the oral pleasures of 'taste sensations' – the repeated action of nibbling away at food (marked by red lipstick).

That the kitchen also evokes childhood memories indexes the relatively unchanging patterns of the familial/maternal life which continue to situate women/mothers in the domestic.[19] Lack of social transformation is arguably a reason for the way in which Baker draws on hysteria as a protest against her domestic 'confinement' . As Catherine Clément explains, the role of the hysteric is both 'anti-establishment and conservative'. 'The hysteric unties familiar bonds, introduces disorder into the well-regulated unfolding of everyday life', and yet 'the family closes around her again'.[20] Performing hysteria, therefore, is a way of marking a protest against domesticity: of disturbing the 'order', the social system which continues to position women within the maternal and the domestic spheres.

Hysteria as Performance

Baker creates a performance register out of a combination of clowning and physical/hysterical markings of the body to relate events, and experiences from her daily life, in a way highly reminiscent of the three-phase 'performance' of *la grande hystérie* by the patients of the nineteenth-century 'expert' in female hysteria, Jean-Martin Charcot.[21] In the final phase of *la grande hystérie*, known as the *attitudes passionnelles*, the patient would mime events and emotions from her life.[22] Similarly, Baker's hysterical marking of her body is a way of 'writing' events, memories, sensations, and emotions associated with the 'madness' of the kitchen.[23]

For example, the first mark in *Kitchen Show* is one in which Baker talks about the ritual of making tea. At the end of this sequence she marks the ritual by binding or bandaging her hand with elastoplast into a teaspoon-holding position. The hand remains thus bound, contorted like the hand of the hysteric, as the performance continues. Each action/mark is posed for the camera; the memory of an event or an emotion is thus written on to the body and 'photographed'.[24]

The last mark, her thirteenth mark – just to make it a Baker's dozen – is to exhibit herself, complete with all twelve marks of ritualized domesticity, on a cake-stand. In presenting herself rather than the meal as the 'product' of her domestic labours, Baker reverses the visibility/status of the food/meal and the invisibility/low status of the woman who labours in the kitchen on behalf of her family.

Moreover, in this final, Charcot-styled pose, she demythologizes the myth of the 'body beautiful'.[25] In offering herself up for visual 'consumption', Baker highlights the way in which food regulates body image for women. Her overalled body is neither streamlined like her cats (as she reminds us with the plastic black bin-liner pegged on to her shoulders), nor can it 'glide' in the blue sky (marked by the blue J-cloths stuffed into and trailing behind her slippers).

Her head is doused in water, her hair is knotted with a wooden spoon, her face is smudged with margarine, and her lips are covered in red lipstick. And yet what is most important, Baker explains to us, is the look which these marks make when they are seen all together. Hysteria, as Elaine Showalter summarizes, is 'a form of expression, a body language for people who otherwise might not be able to speak or even to admit what they feel'.[26] The vocabulary of Baker's thirteenth mark, all her actions put together, articulates the domestic/the 'feminine' body as festival and refusal; writes the 'language' of the kitchen on and through her body both as a celebration of and a protest against 'daily life'.

'Spitting Mad'

One of the dangers in the reception of Baker's work is that the reviewers see only the clowning, not the anger; that they tend, as Claire MacDonald (commenting on *Drawing on a Mother's Experience*) explains, to read her performance only through one self: 'the experienced mother' who makes them 'feel they are in safe hands'.[27] However, in *Spitting Mad*, Baker's short film for BBC2's 'Expanding Picture' series (1997), it is hard to avoid the rage of the maternal. In this 'in-your-face' performance Baker unleashes the anger of the mother which is traditionally silenced by the dominant, caring, nurturing image of maternity.

Briefly, *Spitting Mad* opens with Baker in her garden luxuriating in the fresh, white, linen cloths hanging out on her washing line. A quick tug on a cloth, and we switch to her spotless linen cupboard, where we see Baker taking pleasure in the cleanliness and softness of the neatly stacked washing. From the cupboard we move to a clinical space set with table, chair, and kitchen-style cupboards. The encoding of the clinical again suggests an association between the kitchen and the asylum: a kitchen table and chairs are set in front of a sash window, the bars of which, lit like the furniture in harsh, bright light, link the activity of the kitchen, of food, to madness. In her white overalls Baker signifies both housewife and ('hysterical') patient/inmate.[28]

A white cloth is laid out on a bare table. Baker presents her materials: some household foodstuffs, which variously include oranges, a tin of soup, jams, wine, and sauces. Out of these she proceeds to make a series of five tablecloth paintings. All of the five food paintings are made *via* the mouth, through spitting. In painting number one, Baker chews on orange segments, takes them out of her mouth, squeezes them into the cloth, and knots them into the material with twine.

As she twists and knots the segments into the cloth we note a surge of anger in the action, and the anger mounts through the succeeding four actions/paintings: Weight Watchers tomato soup, sucked up through a straw and blown out onto the cloth to make a lined pattern; strawberry and apricot jams pressed out of her lips onto the cloth; red wine gargled and sprayed out over the cloth; and sauces (yellow and red), chewed and spewed into and onto her 'canvas'. While the paintings start out with patterns (oranges) and lines (soup) the symmetry is upset and distorted by rising anger. Working with the jam painting, Baker abruptly announces that she finds the lines of the lip-shapes of jam pressed onto the cloth boring, and promptly spews out mouthfuls of pink (presumably strawberry) yoghurt to make it more alive.

In the final painting, the camera moves in for a close-up shot as Baker, angrily, tells us that she needs to concentrate to make sure that we get her point. Whereupon she tilts back her head, opens her mouth wide, and pours in the Heinz tomato sauce until her mouth is full, overflowing, and then vomits the red sauce out over the cloth. The anger in this final 'spitting mad' action, signed through the mound of red sauce splattered on the cloth, is especially violent.

It is through the mouth and the symbolism of the regurgitated food that Baker 'speaks' the rage of the mother in *Spitting Mad*. As orifice, opening on/to the body through which food/fluids may pass, the mouth refuses the idea of the bound, pure, proper body, and highlights the abject: the 'dirt', defined in Mary Douglas's terms as 'matter out of place'. 'Where there is dirt there is a system', Douglas argues.[29] Systems of domesticity/maternity are exposed in Baker's film as she upsets the idea we have of the kitchen as a site of cleanliness and hygiene – the idea that anyone preparing food (and, as Baker established in *Drawing on a Mother's Experience* and *Kitchen Show*, traditionally in the family this means the mother) has to be clean, hygienic: in her 'proper' place. Not to obey all the rituals and rules around cleanliness – hand-washing, food-tasting, etc. – is to contaminate, to pollute, to create disorder.[30]

Moreover, the angry regurgitation of food re-visions the 'natural'/nature imagery of the mother who feeds her young in the nest, to suggest not the 'good' mother/breast (in Kleinian terms), but the repressed 'mad'/'bad' mother who fears that she will be sucked dry by the baby/child who must always be fed; and anger, at the way in which, as Coward elucidates, 'domestic relations are ordered around the satisfaction of men's and children's oral needs. Women are expected to nourish not to demand.'[31]

If one takes the Freudian infantile theory of birth in which pregnancy is equated with eating (birth with defecating),[32] then expellation rather than ingestion of food symbolically encodes a refusal of the child/family in the interests of self-nourishment. Or, borrowing from Kristeva,[33] the spitting-out may be read as a means of protecting the self from others – in this case, refusing the maternal self to establish '*myself*', which is especially marked in the spitting out of the Heinz soup (a sign of children's food/meals).

As in *Drawing on a Mother's Experience*, working with the white tablecloths, which become messy through the food painting, gives expression to the way in which a mother's work is a repetitive daily round of tidying, cleaning, and creating order (as in the linen cupboard) only to have the family create disorder, dirt, mess, chaos.

Whereas *Spitting Mad* opens with the clean sheets hung out on the line – lovingly touched and admired by Baker – it closes with a row of 'painted'/'soiled' cloths on display. This 'dirty protest', out in the public space of the garden, is not, however, public enough. Instead, Baker selects two of her paintings/cloths from the line to take with her on a boat on the River Thames. Out on the river she acts as pilot, waving her cloths, signalling in semaphore, to the repeated voice-over, 'Provide better feeding'.

In this, her closing image, Baker is a veritable embodiment of the 'mad', carnivalesque mother. Hers is the 'off-side' maternal body, which Cixous and Clément describe: a dangerous site of disorderly refusal.[34] Like the river (which eventually flows out to *la mère*, sea/mother) she spills out into the city; refuses to be repressed or contained. Baker introduces or 'paints' the 'mad' mother into the foreground of the male-dominated cityscape: Westminster, Big Ben, and the Houses of Parliament are here in the background. 'Provide better feeding', the State's command to mothers, is 'regurgitated' through the food paintings as a feminist demand for the transformation of women's lives: the better provision for and nourishment of a mother's 'daily life'.

Notes and References

1. Hannah Gavron, *The Captive Wife: Conflicts of Housebound Mothers* (London: Routledge, 1966; revised edition, 1983). Gavron committed suicide in 1965, before she had turned thirty.
2. Gavron, *The Captive Wife*, p. 140.

3. Ibid., p. 146.

4. Baker has plans for a further 'Daily Life' show set in a church. During the 1990s she has been performing a series of 'Occasional Tables' – short one-off food performances created for specific events. In this article, my discussion of Baker's performances is based on the video recordings of her shows which are distributed by Artsadmin, London.

5. See Claire MacDonald, 'Feminism, Autobiography, and Performance Art', in Julia Swindells, ed., *The Uses of Autobiography* (London: Taylor and Francis, 1995), p. 187–95; and Deirdre Heddon, 'What's in a Name?', *Studies in Theatre Production*, No. 18 (December 1998), p. 49–59.

6. Lynn MacRitchie, review of *My Cooking Competes*, in Rozsika Parker and Griselda Pollock, eds., *Framing Feminism: Art and the Women's Movement, 1970–1985* (London: Pandora, 1987), p. 230.

7. E. Ann Kaplan, *Motherhood and Representation: the Mother in Popular Culture and Melodrama* (London: Routledge, 1992), p. 6–7.

8. In her autobiographical talk given at the New Works Festival, Leicester, in September 1997, Baker described the three fundamental principles of her work as (1) drawing on her own experiences; (2) working with food; and (3) striving for artistic integrity. Her principle of integrity she explained as her desire that a work of art, a performance, should be 'complete', or 'undiminished' – an almost impossible task, Baker claimed, but one for the artist to aspire to.

9. Quoted from publicity issued by Artsadmin.

10. See, for example, Lynn MacRitchie's review of *My Cooking Competes*, in Parker and Pollock, op. cit.

11. Gavron, *The Captive Wife*, p. 130.

12. Rosalind Coward, 'The Mouth', in *Female Desire: Women's Sexuality Today* (London: Paladin, 1984), p. 121.

13. See Vivien E. Nice, 'Mother to Mother', in *Mothers and Daughters: the Distortion of a Relationship* (Basingstoke: Macmillan, 1992), Chapter 6.

14. It is also interesting to note that in Baker's life-size cake family in *An Edible Family in a Mobile Home*, the baby was modelled on herself, and was significantly the most distressed figure in the familial tableau.

15. Review, *Drawing on a Mother's Experience*, *Performance Magazine*, November 1990.

16. Similarly, in her next show, *How to Shop*, Baker presents the domestic task of shopping through the public discourse of the academic lecture. For a commentary on the kitchen as a private domestic setting used for performance, and the transgressive possibilities which this affords, see Marcia Blumberg, 'Domestic Place as Contestatory Space: the Kitchen as Catalyst and Crucible', *New Theatre Quarterly*, No. 55 (August 1998), p. 195–201.

17. The overalls signify not only domesticity, but also the idea of woman as patient. In *Take a Peek!*, for example, Baker wears several layers of overalls, which are removed, sequence by sequence, to expose social and medical objectification of the female body in a style of grotesque, circus-style, freak-show playing.

18. Caroline Stacey, review of *Kitchen Show*, in *Time Out*, 10–17 July 1991.

19. On this point, see Nancy Chodorow's seminal study, *The Reproduction of Mothering* (Berkeley; Los Angeles: University of California Press, 1978).

20. Catherine Clément, in Hélène Cixous and Catherine Clément, *The Newly Born Woman,* trans. Betsy Wing (Manchester: Manchester University Press, 1987), p. 5.

21. For details see Elaine Showalter, *The Female Malady* (London: Virago, 1985).

22. The first and second phases are the epileptoid phase (the patient losing consciousness and foaming at the mouth); the phase of clownism (the patient producing incredible contortions, distortions of the body); as explained in Elaine Showalter, *The Female Malady,* p. 150.

23. The parallel between Charcot's patients and Baker's own style of hysteria is not lost on Baker herself. Reviewing Baker's show *Take a Peek!*, Marina Warner explained: 'When [Baker] saw the images of herself grimacing, she realized they caught the feeling of the photographs Charcot had taken to illustrate the passions that surfaced in the hysterical condition.' See *The Guardian*, 21 June 1995.

24. Similarly, Charcot would photograph the *attitudes passionelles* of his female patients, and add his own captions as titles (see Showalter, *The Female Malady*, p. 150). In Baker's performances, however, it is she who authors her own image and determines meaning.

25. See Coward, *Female Desire*, p. 37–46.

26. Elaine Showalter, *Hystories: Hysterical Epidemics and Modern Culture* (London: Picador, 1997), p. 7.

27. Claire MacDonald, 'Feminism, Autobiography, and Performance Art', p. 190.

28. See Note 17, above.

29. Mary Douglas, *Purity and Danger: an Analysis of the Concepts of Pollution and Taboo* (London: Routledge, 1966), p. 36.

30. See Douglas, *Purity and Danger*, p. 34.

31. Rosalind Coward, *Female Desire*, p. 119.

32. See Sigmund Freud, *On Sexuality* (Harmondsworth: Penguin, 1977), p. 104.

33. Julia Kristeva, *Powers of Horror: an Essay on Abjection*, trans. Leon S. Roudiez (New York: Columbia University Press, 1982), p. 2–3.

34. See Cixous and Clément, *The Newly Born Woman,* p. 8.

Barnaby King

Landscapes of Fact and Fiction: Asian Theatre Arts in Britain

In the first of two essays which use academic discourses of cultural exchange to examine the intra-cultural situation in contemporary British society, Barnaby King analyzes the relationship between Black arts and mainstream arts on both a professional and community level, focusing on particular examples of practice in the Leeds and Kirklees region in which he lives and works. This first essay looks specifically at the Asian situation, reviewing the history of Arts Council policy on ethnic minority arts, and analyzing how this has shaped – and is reflected in – current practice. In the context of professional theatre, he uses the examples of the Tara and Tamasha companies, then explores the work of CHOL Theatre in Huddersfield as exemplifying multi-cultural work in the community. He also looks at the provision made by Yorkshire and Humberside Arts for the cultural needs of their Asian populations. In the second essay, to appear in NTQ62, he will be taking a similar approach towards African–Caribbean theatre in Britain. Barnaby King is a theatre practitioner based in Leeds, who completed his postgraduate studies at the University of Leeds Workshop Theatre in 1998. He is now working with theatre companies and small-scale venues – currently the Blah Blah Blah company and the Studio Theatre at Leeds Metropolitan University – to develop community participation in theatre and drama-based activities.

It can happen that a civilization can be imprisoned in a linguistic contour which no longer matches the landscape of fact.[1]

THE ARTS COUNCIL'S consultative 'Green Paper', *The Landscape of Fact: Towards a Policy for Cultural Diversity for the English Funding System*, is the most recent incarnation of a very slow development in attitudes towards the provision of arts for ethnic minority groups. Since the devolution of power to the Regional Arts Associations, Arts Council policy no longer directly controls practice, but in two important ways it retains a strong influence: first in that it expresses government attitudes, which the Regional Arts Boards may feel obliged to respond to; and secondly because it still makes broad funding decisions, which are inherently prejudiced in favour of the mainstream arts sector.

The creation of the Arts Council after the war sprang from a sincere desire to 'improve' people by taking culture to them. This culture, packaged and delivered by the state to the people, was essentially identified with the tradition of European high art, which was hierarchically positioned above what might be called 'folk' art – this including all community-based creative activities. The Council's attitudes have developed since those days, but they are still saturated in this paternalistic and imperialist ideology. The arrival of completely *other* traditions of art along with immigrant communities from Asia, Africa, and the Caribbean, posed a deep threat to the Eurocentric tradition of art: they could not easily be incorporated into the mainstream because they derived from completely different aesthetics. The Arts Council's solution was to encourage the concept of 'ethnic arts'.

A report of 1976, entitled *The Arts Britain Ignores*, demanded support for what was then termed 'ethnic minorities' communities' arts', and suggested the structures needed to give such support. As a result of this, the MAAS (Minorities' Arts Advisory Service) was formed, to give advice and training to arts organizations. But a further survey, in 1980, showed that only 0.5 per cent of funding money was being spent on 'ethnic arts', and an 'Ethnic Minority Arts Action Plan' was consequently initiated, which aimed in two years to commit four per cent of Arts Council expenditure to the sector.[2] The target was not reached, mainly due to the lack of a strategic plan for the investment of the money.

The next major policy initiative came in 1989 with a monitoring committee report, *Towards Cultural Diversity*. This was reinforced in 1993 by the publication of *A Creative Future*, which highlighted the need for Black theatre companies to be regularly funded; showed how Black audiences were limited due to perceived discrimination; and how Eurocentric definitions of performance inevitably excluded Black performers.

False Homogeneity – Fallible Diversity

The latest document, *The Landscape of Fact*, is the culmination of much of this work. It recognizes that the level of investment up to now has had little impact, and tries to establish the causes of inequality in the arts sector. It recommends a four-point strategy for development: *access*, to give equal opportunities to Black people to participate in arts activities; *resources*, to give effective, targeted funding; *training*, including job placements and business partnerships; and *infrastructure*, to enable Black arts organizations to gain strength and support from one another.[3]

At face value, these proposals seem both applaudable and comprehensive – but, as I have said, it is Regional Arts Boards who are responsible for implementing such policies in their own regions:

> The purpose of the *Landscape of Fact* exercise was to establish what it is that's causing inequality in the arts sector. It came up with an action plan for key themes. But that sort of work has been going on in the regions for a number of years.
> Sajida Ismail, 7 April 1998

It is not the specific proposals, but rather the broad attitudes as reflected in the terminology and language shifts of Arts Council policy, that actually affect practice, because these have determined the patterns of funding within the sector.[4]

The earliest term used – 'ethnic minorities' communities' arts' – which has an exotic and non-threatening feel about it, regards such artistic production as being rooted in a specific cultural experience and thus of no immediate danger to the mainstream. The obvious association with other forms of 'community arts' further marginalized this. The term 'Black arts', which came to be used more widely in the 'eighties, has a stronger air of political alignment, but nevertheless homogenizes the issue by not differentiating between the many diverse elements it is meant to include – especially between the African–Caribbean and the Asian elements.

Thus the term 'cultural diversity' began to be used as a further concession towards heterogeneity, while attempting at the same time to be inclusive and supportive. It remains, however, a highly problematic term which almost nobody is happy with. *The Landscape of Fact* opens by trying to justify the promotion of 'cultural diversity' in terms of the contributions that Black Arts have made to British culture:

> Black Arts have enriched personal options. . . .
> Black Arts have transformed popular culture. . . .
> Black Arts have brought with them . . . creative influences. . . .
> Black Arts have challenged notions about the place and form of arts. . . .
> *The Landscape of Fact* (1997), p. 5–6

The language gives away the origins of the whole paper – that it is written from the centre, looking out at diverse cultures all around and trying to create patterns out of them. A term such as 'cultural diversity' can never depict all the voices that make up British society and, when unpacked, it turns out to refer to a mass of different groups with different aims and ambitions, both political and artistic. The term cannot hope to embrace the diverse groups within the Asian population, for example, or the continuum which exists between, say, the preservation of a culture's traditions and work which expresses a hybridization between two or more cultures coming together. The 'Green Paper' itself acknowledges that

> Cultural diversity represents a number of often discrete components, with aesthetics that draw, to

differing degrees, on distinctive cultural forms; social, religious, and community functions; generational explorations; and deliberate interculturalism-cultural mixings.

The Landscape of Fact, p. 7

The long passages in the document which attempt to justify and define cultural diversity actually refute the Council's apparent faith in Black artists, since they acknowledge the artistic richness of those cultures but then marginalize them by seeking to fit them into broad categories and definitions in order to deal with them. Effectively, the Black Arts world is denied the ability to grapple for itself with issues of tradition and contemporary culture – this being seen as something which is the responsibility of the arts authorities.

The attitude is reflected in funding policy, which is to deal with Black Arts as a problem issue, discrete from the safe world of white, mainstream arts. Therefore funding for Black Arts is set aside and comes to the RABs principally in the form of Arts Development and Urban Renewal budgets, rather than through the main budgets for regularly funded arts organizations. As a result of this, only two Asian and two African–Caribbean theatre companies are currently working in England.

I would like briefly to shift focus and look at the work of one of these, Tara Arts, to see how Asian theatre workers have been grappling with issues of integration, assimilation and tradition, on their own terms rather than those set by the English funding system.

'Quotation', 'Translation', and Tara Arts

Jatinder Verma, Artistic Director of Tara Arts, is particularly concerned with the expression of Asian identity within a new cultural situation.[5] He argues that it is the nature of the imperialist dominant culture to demonize the *other*, and then to absorb and reduce the *other* to its own image. The legacy of Macaulay's infamous *Note* has outlasted its original context of imperial rule and lives on in the *intra*-cultural politics of modern Britain.

For Verma, as a diasporic Asian, there are two options for the demonized *other*. It can join the club, which would mean conforming and integrating on the terms of the host culture; or it can confront the dominant culture, which represents true interculturalism. Confronting the dominant culture also involves confronting one's own history, and gaining self-knowledge through an awareness of loss. Beyond that there is the challenge to create a new identity, one which is a true reflection of the fragmentary experience of the migrant groups, with its eclectic mix of cultures and influences.

The early work of Tara was based around the experiences of Asians who had come to England *via* East Africa. *Yes, Memsahib*, for example, compared the experiences of the Asian migrant in Kenya and in England, looking at the double displacement suffered by the diaspora communities. However, as Tara's work developed it became more preoccupied with the search for cultural roots in India itself. The company explored traditional Indian forms and symbolically rejected western theatre conventions. This exploration was then brought to bear on a confrontation with European culture, by which means the company dissected traditional canonical texts, using them to set up a dialogue between India and England.

Verma says that the two principal motifs in this work were *quotation*, whereby language and text could represent 'a culture composed of fragments of memory' (Verma, 1997, p. 6), and *translation*, whereby the theatrical text undergoes an experience which is analogous to that of the immigrant, translated from one culture to another.

The essence of *translation*, as exemplified in Tara's production of *Tartuffe*, was thus to adapt the text in such a way that it 'allows the performers to make creative connections between their ancestral traditions and their English present' (Verma, 1997, p. 7). In *Tartuffe* this was achieved partially through the use of a popular theatre tradition of Gujurati, which mirrored the original *commedia* style on which the play was based.

Such creative interactions between cultures are, however, only one part of the work of Asian artists in Britain. Tamasha Theatre Company, an off-shoot of Tara, has chosen a more naturalistic, westernized style of performance in order to present 'slice of life' portrayals of Indian life and of contemporary British–Asian life.

There are three contrasting approaches that have been taken by Asian theatre companies, according to Verma. The first is to present India to England, using western theatre forms so as to raise difficult issues of colonial history and the suffering of Asian people. The second is to present a picture of Asia, but to Asians themselves, here using traditional forms and trying to transport the Asian audience back to the sub-continent in a search for roots. The third and perhaps the most delicate is to employ a creative dialogue between the memory of the Asian migrant and modern England. The latter involves the development of new forms and aesthetics, still culture-specific to the Asian groups involved, but different from the traditional roots they sprang from. This, I would suggest, is interculturalism on one's own terms, not as dictated and orchestrated by the dominant culture of the country.

Asian Arts in the Local Community

Companies like Tara and Tamasha do crucial work in raising the profile of Asian arts in Britain, but evidence suggests that they have relatively little impact on Asian communities in the regions they visit. Tamasha's *A Tainted Dawn*, for example, came to the West Yorkshire Playhouse during the Black Theatre season in October 1997, but played to small, majority white audiences.

Tara have made more effort to visit communities, but in a recent YHA report on South Asian Arts it was stated that 'the drama work and short residencies by Tara Arts in the region were not particularly successful' (Malhotra, 1993, p. 9), the reasons being that not enough effort was made to prepare the ground beforehand, to develop community interest. This is not to devalue the work of Tara, but to suggest that as a national company they are unable to have the close contact and knowledge of a locality which is needed in order to develop Asian participation in the arts. It is in this area that the RABs, such as Yorkshire and Humberside Arts, must take over responsibility from the Arts Council by researching the specific needs of the region, the better to direct its arts provision.

In 1992, the South Asian Arts Forum was initiated by the YHA as a loose network of Asian arts practitioners and organizations, whose primary aims were to advise on the development of Asian Arts strategies and to evaluate their impact. In 1994 the Forum produced a document called '*Aaj-Kal*' *Today and Tomorrow: Context and Recommendations*. Here, it was suggested that training schemes should be established and marketed towards Asians; that major venues should be encouraged to increase South Asian programming; and that Asian arts administrators should be brought into the organization.

Four years on there has been no official survey to evaluate progress, but one positive sign has been the appointment of an Asian Arts development officer, whose job is to identify Asian issues and link them with specific art forms within the YHA. This officer, Sajida Ismail, is highly aware that the problem facing Asian arts is principally one of inequality of opportunity. There is a great wealth of artistic activity in Asian communities, she claims, including orthodox drama work and even some experimental work in multi-media forms. But on the whole there have been very few groundbreaking initiatives, principally because nobody seems to be prepared to invest in allowing Asian artists to take such risks.

Ismail sees this as due to an inherent prejudice in the system, and also a lack of understanding of Asian art forms. Her personal goal is 'to provide a platform for existing South Asian arts work to flourish, which everyone else is allowed. We have to create a level playing field.' This process is about re-education of institutions in the mainstream infrastructure: 'There has to be an integral learning process, otherwise we will make very little movement forward.' Asian organizations must learn the inbuilt inequalities which make it harder for them than for white groups to get funding, and accept that positive action is necessary.

This inequality of access to funding is clearly demonstrated by the fact that most of the arts organizations working with Asian communities are actually white-led, and as such they encounter many stumbling-blocks in working with communities they do not know well. Major Road theatre company, for example, had such difficulties setting up a drama project in Bradford in 1994 that it commissioned a report to look into ways of developing further successful work with the Asian communities in the area.[6] Many important issues were raised by this report, including the common resistance to drama among Asian communities, typified by reactions such as 'our people are not interested in drama' and 'we like to watch, not participate' (Robinson and Singh, 1995, p. 11).

It also seemed that communities had difficulty in accepting outside workers: 'We are a traditional, closed community and we tend to stick within it' (Robinson and Singh, 1995, p. 11). This points to the need for more Asian arts workers, and for arts organizations to access communities through existing structures, such as mosques or schools, rather than contacting them directly.

The main emphasis of the research was on how to work successfully. The problem is not a lack of talent and interest, but rather a lack of research to inform work and resources to support it. The Mehfil report is based on only a very small locality, and it will help local workers in that area, but in a different areas the problems will be different. The only general advice which the report gives is that small initiatives based in real understanding of a community are the only way to proceed effectively:

Ambitious projects will stumble and fall before they are completed. Small steps. We need to be aware of lessons learnt. This will only come about through increased communication, discussion, community consultation and a sharing of good models of practice.
Robinson and Singh, 1995, p. 31

This element of 'sharing good models of practice' seems to me important, since it raises the question of how practices can be documented and evaluated. How easy is it to identify a good model as opposed to a bad one? I would like to look briefly now at a particular model, that of CHOL Theatre company, in order to suggest a way in which its working practice may be analyzed and evaluated against the particular needs of the Asian community.

CHOL Theatre Company

Companies who practise cross-cultural and community-based work are more likely to attract funding than those which do culture-specific work, particularly through sources such as the Single Regeneration Budget (SRB) Challenge fund. The current vogue for urban renewal through cultural activity relies on the power of the arts to create 'confident, imaginative citizens who feel empowered' (Landry *et al.*, 1996, p. 2). The underlying concept and purpose of the SRB are primarily economic, and hence the fund attracts money not only from the government but also from industry and business, in whose interests it is to stimulate economic growth. Money goes to companies like CHOL, who have a good record of high-quality artistic work and a multicultural approach.

So is their approach good for the communities they work with, or just for the companies who give them funding? Adam Strickson, the director of CHOL, emphasizes what he sees as a problematic lack of contact between cultures, which is a root cause of racial tension. His aim is to enable a coming together of cultures through theatre:

It's trying to create original work that reflects a meeting between cultures, which is not just saying you can learn about our culture and we can learn about yours, but it's saying there are these issues, there is this land, this history – what can we say about it now, what forms can we evolve that might draw on Islamic art, on Indian theatre, on the English folk tradition? These forms are new, they are cultural statements for now.
Adam Strickson, 6 January 1998

Such aims seem commendable, but how are they achieved in practice, and do they allow for cultural difference to be maintained?

Based in Huddersfield, CHOL has done work in many areas of Yorkshire. Strickson perceives the work of the company as very much tailored to the needs of those specific communities where they run projects. For them, a community is defined by the mix of people within one geographical location, so when the company begins working in a community, a considerable time is spent on familiarization – identifying different groups and devising ways of bringing them together creatively. The nature of the work in each project is therefore defined by the cultural mix in the area, and the finished 'product' (there always is one) is a creative amalgamation of different cultural groups' creative input.

Though the process often involves drama, the product is not always a conventional performance. *The Riches of the Living Green* was a walk in the Thornhill Lees area of Dewsbury, with an accompanying glossy leaflet with a map, pictures, poems, and other contributions from various – and varied– community groups. Savile Town Youth Club had provided the Islamic texts, a bird bath, and some wooden fish shapes, to be seen on the walk; Howland Centre for the Disabled donated poems and silk leaves; Savile Town Elderly Men's Group had created some designs for the leaflet. This project had the double benefit of bringing diverse elements of the community together, and celebrating the natural beauty of the area. Strickson, however, is realistic about the long-term benefit which such work has:

I've never been convinced by the idea that community workers can go into communities and that in the end communities will be empowered to do it all on their own. We're trying to find ways of empowering people, but it is a very long-term process. . . . Because of the funding situation we can't spend as long as we need to in any one community.
Adam Strickson, 6 January 1998

Because there is neither money for such long-term projects nor for the personal artistic development the company aspires to, a compromise is made whereby every two years the company aims to put together a piece of performance with professional actors, which draws on ongoing community involvement in one or two neighbourhoods. This performance is then toured to other neighbourhoods in the region, along with residencies and workshop programmes which enable the communities to engage in a dialogue with one another, *via* the company.

Images of Transience and Migration

The most recent example of this was *The Bird House*, a potent natural image of transience and migration, but also of safety and refuge. In the publicity it is described as one of three possible events:

A colourful procession of bright plumage followed by multi-lingual stories and songs from England, Poland, Pakistan, and Bangladesh.

A choice of two workshops where groups can either create their own procession or a story for the bird house.

One or two weeks in a village, a city neighbourhood, school, or college creating a sculptural 'bird house' and its stories. The architecture of the house and the content of the stories will reflect the place and people who make them.

Though the work was originally inspired by the refugee experiences of Bangladeshi communities, the final product distances itself from the original subject and achieves relevance for everybody. It also self-consciously involves elements from different cultures, such as puppets, stories and musical instruments. Such work is characteristic of CHOL's aim of 'seeking to develop peace and understanding between people of different racial backgrounds' (CHOL Theatre, 1997), since the work emphasizes similarities and links, and plays down differences and divisions.

The idea of creating art forms to reflect a multiplicity of cultures is open to the criticism that people's own cultural traditions are being exploited for the benefit of the dominant culture. CHOL claims to have 'explored the feelings and history of the minorities, the visionaries, and the neglected' – which I think is true, in that it is, indeed, the company that has explored these areas, rather than letting the minorities explore it for themselves.

CHOL's claim to multiculturalism is thus questionable, because no culturally-specific forms are developed in their own context, but are taken out of context and placed into a new framework – a kind of hybrid performance, which could be seen as a meaningless hotchpotch of cultural activities. In so doing, they place *other* cultures within their own cultural map: rituals and language are taken and replayed in their barest form as theatre.

I would suggest that transfer of culture in this way is validonly if the culture is familiar to you in the first place (as with Tara), so that its basic meanings are accessible and can be faithfully transposed into another cultural milieu. To put it at its simplest and most brutal, the cultural exchange needs to be initiated by the source culture, rather than externally, if it is to not to be an instrument of oppression.

CHOL does not exclude culture-specific work. Strickson acknowledges the need for both kinds of practice, but he is perhaps unaware of the problems that face culturally-specific work, and that the two do not exist on a level playing-field. He is undeniably right that there should be a variety of different kinds of work going on, but at present the funding system doesn't provide for such variety.

Redressing the Balance

Sajida Ismail is very aware of this inequality and it is the primary motivation behind her work at Yorkshire and Humberside Arts:

> We need to recognize that all different ways of working are perfectly valid and legitimate . . . but different methods will work better than others, possibly because the support mechanisms already exist that allow the method to flourish, and give people that confidence to be more experimental in the way they work.

There are a number of reasons for the inequality here identified by Sajida . At the professional end of Asian arts, there is little incentive for artists to stay in the region, due to lack of job opportunities, and many of the more talented artists are drawn to London. Arts organizations are going down because of lack of funding. This is in part due to difficulty in attracting private sponsorship, and also because within the Asian arts sector there is generally much less administrative experience than in the mainstream, which means they are less able to manage finances effectively and make successful bids for lottery funding and the like. This lack of successful professionals in the region has a knock-on effect at a community level: there is little high-quality work to see and few role models for young people to aspire to. Continuing discrimination against Black people in all areas of employment also needs to be more openly acknowledged.

As the development officer for Asian arts, Ismail is responsible for two current initiatives, which seems to me to display more realism and commitment to real change than the politically correct rhetoric of countless Arts Council reports and recommendations. The first is an 'Arts 4 Everyone' lottery bid, to fund an Audience Development Research programme for re-educating venues' programmers, and marketing departments, encouraging them to tap into existing Asian markets and to establish a touring circuit for Asian artists.

The second and larger initiative is a bid to the European Regional Development Fund to set up a Business Exchange, which aims to create partnerships for business training, both for professional arts organizations and for community enterprises. This is a creative equal opportunities initiative to raise skill-levels and to create awareness within the mainstream infrastructure of its own inherent inequalities.

Both these programmes would have tangible and desirable benefits for the Asian communities. For work to be provided on a community level, there needs to be success at a professional level, and this can only come through positive action to redress the financial imbalance. If the bids are unsuccessful, however, the initiatives will be stopped in their tracks, since the budget provided by the Arts Council for development work is minimal, and most of the YHA's annual budget goes to regularly funded organizations, of which very few are Asian.

It is ironic that the successful development of Asian arts provision – something which both the Arts Council and the YHA profess to support wholeheartedly – hangs by a thread. The Arts Council, for all its rhetoric of 'cultural diversity', still pursues a policy of marginalization through funding patterns. The kind of work which allows Asians to explore their identity, represented by companies such as Tara, is thus becoming more sparse rather than increasing. Community-based work, such as CHOL's, tends to be an artistic compromise which plays down cultural specificity, and which can be non-productive if it is not accompanied by sustained culturally-specific work, helping communities explore their own histories and identities.

This may appear to be a simplification of a complex situation, and in some ways it is, but it is in part the failure or refusal of those in positions of power to face some of the simple realities that underly the lack of progress. Realists of clear vision such as Sajida Ismail are valuable, but they are also increasingly frustrated by being forced to bargain for much-needed money.

Notes and References

1. Brian Friel, *Translations* (1981). This quotation is used on the inside cover of the Arts Council document, *The Landscape of Fact* (1997).
2. According to an independent exercise. See Walter Baker, 'The Arts of Ethnic Minorities: Status and Funding' (1985).
3. For details see *The Landscape of Fact*, p. 19–26.
4. 'Appendix 1: The Language Shift', ibid., p. 32–5.
5. See Verma, 1996; and Verma, 1997.
6. Sara Robinson and Harmage Kalari Singh, *Major Road: the Mehfil Project Report* (1995). This report was the result of three months of research, including face-to-face interviews and meetings. The quotations given are comments made by Asian people in response to specific questions by the researchers, which are documented in the report.

Gavin Carver

The Effervescent Carnival: Performance, Context, and Mediation at Notting Hill

The Notting Hill Carnival is now Europe's largest street festival, celebrating the music and popular arts of a variety of cultures. Not so long ago, the event – which sometimes culminated in violence between the police and carnival goers – was widely perceived as both threatening and marginal. But more recently the size, success, and high media profile of the carnival have given it a 'responsible' image – and won sponsorship from a variety of commercial concerns. In this article Gavin Carver explores these developments in the mediation and context of the carnival, and asks whether the sponsorship has contributed towards the containment of the carnival, transforming a socio/cultural event into mere decorative spectacle. Gavin Carver is a Lecturer in Drama at the University of Kent.

IN 1995 the Notting Hill Carnival, held annually in London at the end of August, was sponsored by Lilt, a brand of soft, fizzy, tropical fruit-flavoured drink manufactured by Coca-Cola, and became the Lilt Notting Hill Carnival, an arrangement that continued in 1996 and 1997. In 1998 the carnival was sponsored by Virgin Atlantic, who supported the event for that year only, after Nestlé, who were to have taken over, withdrew their support. The 1999 carnival, sponsored by Western Union, was duly restyled the Western Union Notting Hill Carnival.

This article considers the manipulation and commodification of the carnival, focusing specifically on the Lilt sponsorship – the first and longest, and so currently the most culturally significant, of the named sponsorships.[1] The name *Lilt Notting Hill Carnival* seems to embody so many of the contradictions and ambiguities that have been the subject of much writing about carnival and the carnivalesque. For carnival is a difficult beast, existing in tension between its radical and conservative tendencies – its ability to challenge, mock, and even change social norms weighed against its function as safety valve: a joyful, cathartic release in whose aftermath the world returns to normal.

Its apparent opposition to sobriety and authority is checked by the need (in modern carnival at least) for it to be well organized, deemed safe, funded, and licensed. Its operation as a deeply felt cultural and political performance is entwined with its obvious role as entertainment of the most visceral and popular kind. Carnival offers a glimpse of alternative life strategies, indexing values and behaviour that may be found threatening or at least distasteful by the dominant classes. Since true carnival offers a vision and reworking of the world as seen from below, the hegemonic order of any one era attempts to control carnivalesque expression, orienting it towards its harmonious and cathartic functions while eliminating its radical or revolutionary potential.

The commercial sponsorship of the Notting Hill Carnival highlights a number of critical problems, both for the specific event and carnival in general. These arrangements are the latest developments in the growth of the festival from its small beginnings in 1966 to its current position as Europe's largest street festival. The increasing popularity of the carnival is such that the organizers have considered moving it at least partly out of Notting Hill to become a London-wide event.

In many ways it is easy to see the sense of the sponsorship arrangement: the carnival is growing in size and facing increasing costs; it attracts media attention and presents itself as Europe's biggest party with an 'exotic' slant; it offers a potential advertiser a perfect carnival image. However, twenty years ago the carnival presented extraordinary scenes of violence generally regarded as far more than festive excess taken to unfortunate extremes. The history of the carnival has always been balanced between cultural resistance and incorporation – a knife-edge common to many festive practices, few of which, however, have so high a profile as the carnival at Notting Hill. One wonders whether the recent developments represent a final act of incorporation, whether this festival devoted to 'strength through liberation and culture'[2] is falling victim to the totalitarianism of western capitalist society?

Background to the Carnival

There is nothing particularly new about the commercialization of subcultural forms – notably, of late, many apparently oppositional music styles and their attendant fashions such as rap and punk with its (degraded or upgraded?) appearance on catwalks and postcards. The process by which this takes place is both economically and culturally motivated, as commercial interests become aware of a street style or subcultural form generated within a local and specific context. In order to exploit the form they have to generalize the context, removing it from its roots so that it may appeal to a wider audience and be disseminated through respectable media.[3]

In the process such alternative cultural events are bounded by what are hegemonically established to be appropriate aesthetic and political parameters, thus depriving the form of its original oppositional or counter-cultural voice. A wealth of critical writing has discussed the complexity of this relationship, developing the sense that subcultural forms depend upon condemnation to index their oppositional status and can only evade commercialization by a continuous reworking of mass-produced artefacts and mutation of their own identity.[4]

The carnival, which is largely based on West Indian (specifically Trinidadian) traditions, takes place over August Bank Holiday weekend. Sunday is dedicated to the children's carnival, the carnival proper being on the Monday. Estimates suggest that over the two days something over one million people occupy what is a very small area of London. There is an enormous procession involving steel bands and walking participants, all dressed in extraordinary colourful costumes, some of which are effectively huge puppets. These costumed participants belong to *mas* (short for masquerade) bands, each of which bases its designs around a particular theme. In 1995 there were 67 such bands – 150 being claimed by 1998. In addition to the procession there are several static sound systems

(50 in 1995) in the side streets around which carnival-goers dance, three stages for live performance (one sponsored by BBC Radio One), and a host of vendors selling food, drink, and carnival paraphernalia.

Since its birth eight years after the 1958 race riots in Notting Hill, the carnival has always offered challenge and always been contested.[5] Originally a small local festival, it was intended to promote mutual understanding among the polyethnic population of the area and to enhance the image of what had been a disreputable area of London. But even in its early years the event was regarded with suspicion by the authorities, since it was seen to offer a united voice for the poor of the area, who, white or black, were caught in an appalling housing situation. Indeed, the first carnival had civic sponsorship withdrawn by the local Mayor, since the event was believed to have a subversive element.[6]

The Necessity for Cultural Appeasement?

The context of the carnival, mobilizing the local working class, could not help but give it a political content. By the 'seventies the carnival had become an almost entirely West Indian event – initially Trinidadian, but in time involving Jamaican participants, most notably through the inclusion of sound systems.[7] Its identity became entwined with the situation of West Indians in Britain, who saw themselves as the victims of a white authoritarian culture. It was against this background of opposition and the growth of attendance at carnival that the riots of 1976 took place, initiated, it is generally agreed, by high-profile police action against street traders and year-long arguments between the police and the carnival organizers.

Since 1976 the organising body of the carnival has become increasingly and perhaps necessarily concerned with enterprise and cultural appeasement, but this has been achieved in the face of some opposition that has denounced the carnival for selling out West Indian heritage and identity. The conflict over the ideological direction of carnival was perhaps most evident in the two years following 1976, when two rival organizations with differing philosophies attempted to control the event.[8]

Not all carnivals since 1976 have been peaceful. Further violent clashes thus took place in 1987, brought about by a number of opportunistic crimes and police action that was perceived as being heavy-handed. Since that year, however, the carnival has become increasingly contained both physically and ideologically – partly due to its sheer scale, but also to the position it has come to occupy. Its status as Europe's largest street festival not only points to an event whose preparations require professional, well-orchestrated planning, but also marks it out as being part of a respectable cultural menu.

In 1989 the management body became a limited company, determined to negotiate a path for the carnival that would allow it to assume a multi-cultural London identity while staying true to its West Indian roots. Five years before the sponsorship arrangement, Robert Hewison was already observing that even the 'spirit of carnival . . . must be accommodated to the enterprise culture'.[9] In 1997 the organizing body became a charitable trust.

The carnival increasingly appears to be a festival of street art and a general celebration of popular creativity rather than a wholly culture-specific event. The carnival procession of 1995 included amongst many others a band from Switzerland, a float from Bognor Regis, and many Brazilian participants. In addition to the conscious decision to push the carnival in a more multi-cultural direction, many of the participants are of a generation born in Britain, 'so they're bringing to carnival their Britishness, their Englishness and we absorb that into carnival. That is another stage in our evolution as a people. We are here in London and we have to reflect that.'[10]

London is more polyethnic than Trinidad (hence the inclusion of Jamaican traditions, which would not occur in the Trinidad carnival) and Claire Holder, as present chief executive of the trust (and previously Chair of Notting Hill Carnival Ltd.), is determined that the event should reflect cultural diversity rather than appear as a monolithic West Indian event; but however multi-cultural it may become there is an underlying reference to a black cultural heritage inscribed within the carnival.

The Notting Hill carnival is essentially an occasion when many black people come together to assert their presence culturally, politically, socially and, if needs be, violently, in symbolic affirmation of the mood of agitation endemic to the existence of black people in an overwhelmingly white milieu.[11]

Political Weight, Decorative Spectacle

Abner Cohen[12] has ably demonstrated that 'although it is essentially a cultural, artistic spectacle, saturated by music, dancing, and drama', the Notting Hill Carnival 'is always political, intimately and dynamically related to the political order and to the struggle for power within it'.[13] The difficulty with any analysis of carnival is this double aspect, the political and the entertaining, which manifests itself through a dialogue between two 'meaningful' strata.

On one level the performance of carnival is apparently semiotically transparent, presenting culturally resplendent artefacts in a context of celebration; this transparency is of course subject to the context of the observer, but on the level of appearances the meaning-making is decoded as 'artistic spectacle'. Costumed groups depict stories/themes that may be connected, often tangentially or metaphorically, to West Indian identity, but are dominated by the spectacular manner of their telling. There is certainly nothing didactic in most *mas* presentation,[14] and the response is generated on a visceral rather than intellectual level, relying on rhythmic music, lavish costumes, colour, and dance. 'To the inexperienced eye this panoramic view reveals a kinaesthetic construct: a dancing explosion of myriad patterns of every colour.'[15]

However, this spectacular performance of carnival is serious because of the second layer of meaning that exists underneath it: the cultural and critical context. As Beckerman has observed, a spectacular image is often bereft of clear significance, but the meaningful component may be lacking a spectacular manifestation:[16] it is the dialogue between the spectacular and the significant that gives an event magic and meaning. In the case of the Notting Hill Carnival the contextual 'weight' or significance is provided by the history of West Indian immigration to Britain, of slavery and emancipation, and of the original Trinidad carnivals – not to mention the discourses of carnival critique as exemplified by Bakhtin.

The grounding to the Notting Hill carnival, why it has to be taken seriously and will always be taken seriously, is not the politics from recent times but the reasons why carnival happened in the first place. Carnival happened because of the liberation and whenever you are in an environment where there is oppression that is there in the background.[17]

Interestingly (and crucially), although it is these contextual concerns that provide the cultural weight to the surface performance, they are not always specifically denoted in the performance text. The weight is the unspoken subtext and context of carnival, the known rather than the articulated.

Occasionally the context of the carnival makes its way to the surface; in 1986 the Mangrove[18] *mas* presentation was themed 'Me Myself, I Warrior', uniting the oppressed peoples of the world under the communal banner of 'warrior'. On the other hand, in 1974 a theme was 'A Visit to Disney Land'.[19] More recently, in 1995, themes ranged from 'Celebration' to 'Exotica' to 'Rituals of the Sioux Indians' – the last partially connecting the experiences of another oppressed warrior nation, but equally revelling in the exotic and the fantastic, and certainly distanced from local experience and imagery.

Indeed, of the thirty-seven *mas* bands who gave an account of their theme in the *1996 Touch Carnival Guide*,[20] only five presented themes that might be regarded as overtly representative of the politics of West Indian heritage,[21] a further fourteen were loosely culturally motivated, usually depicting 'multi-coloured' themes, while the remaining eighteen presented themes that were largely decorative spectacle.

purest sense, it is difficult to reconcile with a carnival that exists as much for its spectators and the media, particularly when the intention is to be multi-cultural. In short, *mas* spectacle has only a limited transparency, and is dependent upon the reader having some knowledge of it references. In a sense the weight of carnival is provided by an awareness of the history of breach and crisis[24] within the black community, while the spectacular performance celebrates and symbolizes a reincorporation into a new order of emancipation; however, in order for the latter to be effective, knowledge of the oppression must be present. To this we shall return.

The relationship between cultural context and spectacular performance is therefore highly problematic, since the carnival is generated from an Afrocentric perspective but appropriated, mediated, and legislated upon within a Eurocentric forum. It is because of these widely differing understandings of carnival that genuine exchange is impossible, since all referents within the exchange are contingent upon the cultural and historical position of the speaker or audience.

If one accepts the stratification of carnival into context and spectacle, then it is quite an easy step to imagine how the manipulation of the relationship between the two levels could affect the nature and reception of the carnival event. Effectively – and this is the primary concern of this article – circumstances may separate or unbalance the constituent parts leading to decontextualized performance (decorative entertainment?) or 'weight' without rehearsed and ritualized expression (riot or non-event?). Umberto Eco has drawn attention to this very phenomenon in his essay on carnival, where he suggests that a situation of 'unexpected or non-authorized carnivalization' may be regarded as revolution.[25]

Performer and spectator, art and life mix in an event that may be read and written as either, or both, spectacular entertainment or a deeply political contest. The *mas* bands are both an aesthetically beautiful manifestation of West Indian visual traditions and a clear

Tensions between Context and Spectacle

Patricia Alleyne-Dettmers has provided a useful critique of the meaning-making in carnival *mas* imagery. Her term meta-mask suggests the contemporary reworking of historically and culturally diverse *mas* images to provide 'a powerful vehicle for restoring and revising the fragmented Trinidad/Afro–Caribbean historical past – its ancestral voices'.[22] In a detailed analysis of one *mas* presentation, she illustrates this appropriation and celebratory representation and suggests that it offers finally 'a new and positive vision of [Caribbean] history'.[23] While such specific significance is clearly present within many *mas* performances, their reading depends upon an awareness, sometimes quite specialized, of that history, and as such is of principal significance to the *mas* performers themselves.

Although this participant-centred significance is true to the idea of carnival in its statement about the right of that culture to a place on the street and in the national cultural discourses, whether or not the imagery is explicit.

Carnival is a street festival because the slaves could not walk the streets after dark without their white masters. When those laws were repealed we took to the streets in song and dance . . . and that is what we celebrate in Notting Hill, the right, the freedom to be on the streets.[26]

Ideological Transactions, Cultural Price

Carnival allows a time of release and excess, a symbolic rebellion from the normally imposed social restraint; it is a celebration of the irrational and the Dyonisian in the face of 'official culture's claims to authority, stability, sobriety, immutability, and immortality'.[27] This opposition is sharpened since the carnival is a celebration of culture erupting on the streets of London, an architectural embodiment of the supremacy of capitalist rationality. It does not need to be overtly political: the presence of one million people taking to the streets, subverting their everyday use, undermining their functionality, is a political act in itself, particularly when a significant proportion of those are black.[28]

Streets that are normally devoted to the daily routine of life (consumption, production, transportation, and habitation) are thus taken over or mutated to become a site of the extraordinary and the excessive. One must not lose sight, however, of the fact that the extraordinary and the excessive are also bound up in commercial as well as cultural transactions: for carnival pleasures are also a commodity.

The carnival, as Bakhtin, followed by Stallybrass and White, have suggested,[29] is firmly located in the market-place, with all its twentieth-century capitalist connotations. Indeed, carnival time does not so much challenge the daily commerce of the street as absurdly escalate it, allowing traders (licensed and otherwise) to sell their wares at inflated prices on pitches sold to them (in the past at least) by the carnival organizers. With titled sponsorship, the identity of the carnival itself has also proved to be a commodity.

The symbolic and, importantly, the actual struggle for the street is central to the operation of carnival – and it was this battle that was directly responsible for the violence of the 1976 carnival. Carnival claims the street for its participants, the state claims that the street is under its control and seeks to ensure that behaviour is always 'appropriate'.[30] The carnival now operates under a curfew that requires the streets to start being cleared at seven o'clock – which has clear echoes of the position of the slaves in Trinidad. Thus, although the organizers understandably claim that the curfew is a practical necessity, the lines between freedom and containment are by no means clear. It is interesting to note that, in general, violent occurrences at the Notting Hill Carnival take place towards the end of the weekend, suggesting that as reincorporation is imminent the *communitas* of carnival makes one last assault on the *structure* of authority.[31]

The curfew, the police presence, and local authority containment of the event are all part of the narrative of the performance, since a return to the status quo is enshrined within the script of carnival. 'Lent' must arrive, and the streets have to return to their daily use. Indeed, the form of a procession, which is at the heart of the carnival, clearly indicates the temporary nature of the crisis, since a procession must, by definition, terminate; it is spatially and temporally bounded. This closure is symbolically attested by the presence of the police, and acknowledged in the form of the event.

The carnival may, however, be perceived not only as a two-day event, but also as one lasting thirty-five years; and over this period a similar process of reincorporation may be seen to have taken place. On a macro-level the riots of 1976 may be seen to be a crisis of great magnitude after a growing breach between organizers and authority, and the years since have witnessed increased efforts at containment and normalization. It was unavoidable that after the events of 1976 the carnival had to reposition itself or face abolition, for in England the Home Secretary has the power to ban such an event. The repositioning has taken place through a process of dialogue and exchange, as here described by Holder:

Carnival was growing beyond all expectations, so that if it continued to grow in a political way it would be a serious problem, so the political element had to be diffused in some way. And the only way to diffuse it was by understanding the culture. . . . So the police would talk with the carnival committee not just about crowd management but about culture. In the 'eighties exchanges started happening.[32]

Although such ideological transactions are necessary to ensure the physical safety of carnival and thus its continued existence, there is, potentially, a cultural price. As the breach between carnival body and official body is narrowed or obscured, the spectacle becomes decontextualized and the resultant ritual may be resituated as decorative entertainment. *Pace* Kershaw,[33] these transactions may achieve a quiet efficacy in reaching mutual understanding, but run the risk of disempowering the symbolic content of the spectacle.

Darcus Howe, political commentator and one-time chair of the carnival, has suggested that 'if the knowledge of carnival as a struggle dies, the carnival as it was conceived is in danger of dying'.[34] This position holds that carnival was born out of struggle and that it stands as a monument to (and performance of) that conflict. Once it operates with equanimity, the deeply political nature of West Indian cultural heritage is lost from view. But Howe's position, desirable or otherwise, is untenable. The process of negotiation, exchange, and containment is a process of attrition that has affected the operation of carnival throughout history. Carnival either succeeds in its critical or indeed revolutionary quest, thus making itself redundant, or it is eventually (and far more often) contained to a point where it functions in support of the status quo: to borrow from Marcuse, 'the achievement cancels the premise'.[35]

Carnival as Commodity

In general emphasis has been placed on the containment of carnival through force, legislation, reform, or temporal bounding. However, there is a further process which has more recently worked itself out in carnival: the pervasiveness of manipulation by the mass media of cultural artefacts and their symbiotic relationship with popular culture.

Commercial sponsorship is the latest event in this process of cultural exchange affecting the carnival. That it took place at all is testament to the increasingly 'good' public image of the carnival, and its effect is likely further to confirm that image. On the one hand the organizers are keen to present such an impression, since the carnival is the most high-profile black cultural event in Europe, and it is important that it not only offers scenes of wild celebration and cultural solidarity, but also testifies to the competence and responsibility of the organizing group. As Holder says, 'The carnival is a vehicle for black credibility. The authorities used to try to ban it, saying it was dangerous, but we have shown that we take accountability very seriously.'[36]

Within traditional carnival discourses this may appear paradoxical, but I suggest that one of the conservative devices of carnival is that it presents its participants as wild, dangerous, and irresponsible, hence vindicating the leadership of the dominant order. Indeed, Gutzmore goes so far as to suggest that the problems faced by the management crises of 1976 to 1978 were, at least in part, externally engineered,[37] thanks to the creation of a mythology of disorganization, radicalism, and lack of ideological cohesion – an obvious target for redressive action.

Carnival keeps those below in their place since they are presented as unworthy of any other position. On the other hand, if carnival presents itself as a managerially competent body, creating a cultural image that may appear less radical but which diffuses accusations of marginality, it becomes a viable cultural alternative. There is, however, a price to pay, and for obvious reasons there was opposition to the arrangement.[38]

Firstly there was the new name: *The Lilt Notting Hill Carnival*. The most significant implication is the ascription of authorship. The title Notting Hill Carnival situated the carnival in an area which contained a concentrated and disadvantaged black population in the 'fifties, and which was the site of race riots in 1958; it also subtly created an interesting dialectic, since Notting Hill was becoming increasingly popular with trendy, middle-class, and yuppie residents. The Notting Hill Carnival signifies a non-specific communal authorship, bound by a common socio-political identity, and it firmly ascribes a local character to the carnival – whatever the commercial truth might be, it suggests that the carnival is a local production of participatory pleasures in opposition to the imposed pleasures of the culture industry.[39]

The 'Lilt' Connection

Whilst the original name remained, the carnival was intrinsically tied to the area, both physically and semiotically. The fact that a brand name now prefixes the location ascribes the authorship (and by implication ownership) to a very specific corporate body rather than to a demographic and social context, and redefines the struggle for the streets as bureaucratic negotiation rather than political contest. It is not hard to see how the eventual end product might be the Western Union Carnival in Hyde Park.[40]

That the reference to authorship is far more explicit than that of the original title by implication shifts the event from being a social *and* aesthetic drama to being purely an aesthetic one, since the presence of an author is a clear indication that the drama is both rehearsed and contained.[41] In keying or reframing the Notting Hill Carnival as a commercially oriented entertainment, Lilt in consequence inevitably obscured the weight. The foregrounding of a product is in direct conflict with carnival's emphasis on the bodily principle: for carnival liberates the bodily pleasures of 'the other', most particularly of the young, and further still of young West Indians. It demonstrates an autonomy of the individual and communal body which challenges both the sensibilities of puritanical culture and the subjugation of the body by legislation and capitalist production. Lilt clearly reaffirmed the dominant status of commodity, and comfortably situated the carnival within a culture of *gesellschaft*.

Lilt has a brand image, and the first irony that strikes one is that Lilt is a non-alcoholic drink. Carnival is a time of excess and corporeal indulgence, a time of letting go and licence, whereas the sponsor offers an image of joyful 'sobriety'.[42] The riots of 1976 which situated the carnival as a deeply political and oppositional voice were partly initiated by an argument over selling alcohol on the streets – the organizers arguing that the consumption of alcohol at carnival was traditional and that the British establishment should respect this cultural tradition, the establishment holding that it should not.

The presence of Lilt appears to signal capitulation to a culture of relative sobriety. Lilt presents itself as a tropical fruit drink, capturing exotic flavours in a can; its appeal resides in this taste of the Caribbean. Carnival, throughout its history in this country, has attempted to reposition itself away from the merely exotic and represent itself as a vocal part of the whole polyphony of British culture[43] – while ironically Lilt, through its television advertising, had rejected British imagery in favour of a stereotyped version of the Caribbean as a vacation resort offering a carefree lifestyle. This advertising imagery of sea, palm trees, and a laid-back attitude to life are highly reminiscent of commercials for holiday destinations. This does not so much depoliticize West Indian heritage as re-present it. The semiotic implications of the Virgin Atlantic sponsorship are no less problematic, since Richard Branson, founder and Chief Executive of the Virgin group of companies, owns his own Caribbean Island.[44]

Lilt depended upon the spectacle of the carnival rather than its context, the latter being both irrelevant to the product and possibly damaging to its identity. The corollary of this is that the carnival must emphasize festive aspects over context in order to maintain the sponsorship. Many observers have illustrated that the use of subcultural forms by mass media has both occasioned and depended upon the relocation of the form away from its originating context.[45] This may be seen as the removal, or at least the obfuscation of the ancestral voices of breach, and thus the social/cultural divisions that provide the context of the carnival crisis.

Consumerism and Carnival

This is achieved in part by the retitling of the event, but more significantly through the manipulation of the image of carnival in the minds of carnival-goers – and equally importantly those who watch from a distance. The identity of the promoted and the promoting become increasingly entangled, as through its media presence Lilt may have inflected the reception of carnival, locating it in the realm of the exotic while promoting an image of pluralism and racial harmony.

Lilt's image and campaign did not stand alone, but existed within an intertextual framework of other promotional campaigns which utilize the carnival trope.[46] As Robert Stam observes, the carnival metaphor is used time and time again as a vehicle for product/ideology promotion, and its prominent presence in the media must construct a widely disseminated image of carnival that is linked to consumer excitement, working for, rather than offered as an alternative to, the routine of production and consumption.

Such manufactured images of carnival are devoid of context or dissent: they are, in Stam's words, 'weak, truncated, and ersatz'.[47] The ideology presented is one of a world 'without work, social conflict, or indeed any socially negative features at all'.[48] This is the strength of corporate promotional culture – a culture that is quite capable of reinventing carnival for its own purposes (as it has done frequently). Carnival is presented not as a social utopia but a permanent sun-drenched holiday– people dancing in the streets in a context that is entirely depoliticized.

Lilt's campaign, like those of other carnival commodities, thus had a clear message: drink Lilt and it will take you to paradise. Ironically, of course, those who initiated the Notting Hill Carnival left 'paradise' to find work in Britain. The apparent multi-cultural liberalism of Lilt's campaign (still on-going after their sponsorship deal terminated) has a strong hint of 'feel-good colour-blindness' that appeals to a particular group of affluent, middle-class liberals,[49] although, as noted above, a number of *mas* presentations also referred to this rainbow ideology.

In the week of 1–7 July 1996, Lilt placed four advertisements on nationwide Channel Four television, and two or three (varying between locations) on regional ITV stations. Channel Four is (or was then) the minority and 'intellectually' oriented station designed to appeal to Wernik's affluent middle-class liberals. One of the Channel Four commercials fell aptly in the middle of *Friends* – a sitcom of witty, middle-class, attractive, white twenty-somethings. A second followed just twelve minutes later, between *Friends* and *Frasier* – another sitcom, featuring a highbrow analyst. Lilt, through the carnival (and the carnival by association with Lilt) was communing with the very people who should have felt threatened by its inversions, and it did so by utilizing the rainbow-world performance of carnival at the expense of its oppositional weight.

Conservatism in the Land of Cockaigne

A further use of the carnival as a media stage or conduit of communication was the appearance of the recently elected Conservative leader, William Hague, and his then fiancée, Ffion Jenkins, at the carnival in 1997. Hague came complete with whistle. This was not an official visit intended to observe the cultural significance of the carnival: he attended to be photographed having a good time and being youthful and 'of the people'. Arguably in true carnival spirit, the high attempted to become low.

There were many carnival inversions and paradoxes in this appearance. Steve Pope observed tartly that the Conservative Party had done 'nothing to improve the lot of black people in this country',[50] while the Criminal Justice Act of 1994, brought in by the Conservatives, sought to criminalize gatherings not dissimilar to the carnival. This, while being seen as hypocritical by some, is clearly close in spirit to the early modern period's vindication of carnival by authority, a practice that both allowed a space for the populace to vent their frustrations and energies in a structured way (a safety valve), and demonstrated the good natured magnanimity of the leadership in allying themselves with the carnival body. Hague's move may have had few supporters, but it had historical precedent.

However, the corporate carnival is seemingly at odds with the original ideology of carnival where the poor mocked the rich, and where those below were king. If there is a similarity, it is in the excessive emphasis on consumption of one kind or another, although early carnival mocked the status and cost-value of commodities. Ladurie reports that in the 1580 carnival in Romans the prices of food were reversed so that luxuries were cheap and bread expensive.[51] During the 1995 Notting Hill Carnival a brand of drink in competition with Lilt called Liptonice (manufactured by Pepsi) was handed out free to members of the crowd in an ironic variation on the Land of Cockaigne, the carnival realm of free-flowing wine and food – here offered as subversion of commodity value in the cause of product promotion. Lilt did not comment.

In 1992 the carnival organizers estimated that twelve million pounds would be spent by carnival-goers during the two days.[52] Carnival cannot be separated from consumption of commodities but, unlike the utopian vision of carnival, the free market dictates that at carnival time all goods are sold at inflated prices.

Carnival is a potentially subversive form, but one that is very seductive; for commercial reasons as much as cultural, the form is transfunctionalized or reinvented by mass culture and repositioned through its mainstream dissemination. Whether such transfunctionalizing has actually happened to the Notting Hill carnival is less significant than that it has happened to the idea of carnival in general, the identity of which is being restructured by advertising semiosis. Lilt, Virgin Atlantic, William Hague, and Western Union are clearly part of the mainstream culture: their condoning of the event through the media – and more importantly the dialogic synthesis of the carnival sign and the corporate sign – communicates, prior to the event itself, that the carnival represents cultural balance and equanimity.

Wernick demonstrates throughout his study of *Promotional Culture* 'that the extension of promotion throughout all circuits of social life is indeed a force for cultural homogenization'.[53] Where carnival is a celebration of disorder and polyphony, of the world turned upside down, corporate promotion seeks to normalize and order – not least into the ABC of classes so dear to market research.

Once the breach is masked, the carnival crisis appears unfounded or decontextualized. The contest of the streets may come to be seen as a bureaucratic and commercial endeavour rather than a deeper social and symbolic conflict. And once this contest is nullified, the *mas* presentations and steel bands become cultural reductions rather than indices of deeper cultural issues. More importantly, the reframing of the drama as purely aesthetic removes any discourse that might accommodate discussion of the more excessive or violent transgressions, which are a central part of carnival. Effectively, any manifestation of the *communitas* acting against the law may quite easily be reduced to mindless criminality, since without the breach or weight there appears to be no context for social crisis; crisis simply does not fit with the Lilt (or Coca-Cola) culture.

Carnival has had an immense impact on popular culture, whether through the three S's of multi-culturalism (samosas, saris and steel bands) or its exploitation in postmodernism. But if we examine popular cultural notions of carnival we find remnants of a colonial fantasy ranging from the racist to the liberal and including a repertoire of stereotypes from the non-threatening exotic event of jollification to a congregation of threatening 'savage' criminals.[54]

The representation of carnival-goers may now be broken down into two polarized stereotypes: those not fitting into the palatable exercise of jollification are thus easily dismissed as savages once the frame of the event is shifted to decontextualize the crisis. The carnival becomes a public-relations exercise, making 'empty multi-racial gestures as media photo opportunities'.[55]

A survey of *The Times* from 1976 to 1994 reveals a fairly consistent pattern of reporting. If the event is 'trouble free' it receives brief coverage, sometimes including a photograph – like the one opposite, depicting a black child carried on the shoulders of a policeman.[56] If, however, the event ends in violence, the news coverage tends to be more extensive and focuses primarily on the carnival as a policing problem and as an index to our violent times.[57] In either case the emphasis is on the maintenance of law and order, and the efficacy of reincorporation.[58]

The representation of carnival is caught between two mediating forces, both of which focus their transformations primarily but not exclusively on youth culture. The entertainment angle of promotion foregrounds the spectacular aspects but removes the weight; the news-media angle emphasizes the dominant culture's closure of the event and constructs a simplified view of the operation of the carnival: it becomes, like the EPCOT Centre, a reduction of culture to costumes and food and a Disney reworking of culture,[59] or, in mainstream news, a discourse on the sovereignty of the status quo.

Musical Resistance

Pryce argues that the resisting element of carnival is primarily to be found in its advocacy of a youth subculture.[60] However, it is this particular element of cultural expression that is most prone to essentializing or decontextualizing by the media which claim to speak for it. Thus, the vast majority of news coverage focuses on describing and explaining the activities of black youths who are generally constructed as 'the problem' of the carnival. Additionally, media transfunctionalizing of subcultural objects such as music and style is clearly centred upon youth culture.

Lilt (like Hague) used the youthfulness of carnival to sell its product, whose primary targeted consumers are sixteen- to twenty-four-year-olds (as is the case with all carbonated drinks). Crucially, it is not simply carnival as such that is the site of media containment but specifically the youth contingent – the very group that, according to Pryce, has the ability to 'transform the symbolic resistance power manifested at carnival time into actual political power in the British state'.[61]

The focus of youth interest and activity at the carnival is not the procession itself, but the sound systems that occupy the streets near the procession route. Space forbids the exploration of those sound systems in any depth in this article, but critiques of British and American black popular music, of which there are many, provide appropriate analyses which may be applied to these phenomena.

It is worth noting that music, like carnival, exists in a complex and partially symbiotic relationship with commodity culture, and that in the final analysis critics are less than convinced that mass media makes impotent

the music and the style of counter-cultural groups, but suggest rather that each continually critiques the other.[62] However, when primarily black music, formulated from disempowered and counter-cultural positions, is played within the increasingly gentrified streets of Notting Hill, its destabilizing status becomes clear.

These sound systems foreground the body in almost erotic display through dancing. With rap and reggae, the language spoken or sung over the music utilizes subcultural argot (billingsgate) and the words and forms may be specifically oppositional, sometimes foregrounding the experience of poverty and of oppression. Additionally, the music played by the sound systems and the culture that it promotes is precisely that which the recent Criminal Justice Act has attempted to control, thus adding a specifically targeted political critique to the event. The sound system is central to the weight of carnival, which throughout its history in this country 'has added a cutting edge to its site of cultural political contestation'.[63]

Interestingly, however, the carnival guide of 1996 quotes the advice of Mike Anthony, a carnival DJ, on how to please the crowd: 'No swearing on the mic., don't speak about politics, religion, or race, those things don't even come into it.'[64] Additionally, much of the music of choice for many of the sound systems is no longer solely the overtly oppositional reggae, calypso (central to traditional carnival), or rap, but now includes jungle, chutney soca, or other forms whose meanings are made opaque by their more frivolous lyrics or even absence of words, only open for decoding by the culturally educated.

Perhaps it is the sense of *communitas* generated by understanding and responding to these musical forms and their euphemisms that is more potent than a defined political content.[65] Certainly, lyrics are not necessary to point to the association of these sound systems and their play-lists with illegal raves – and the allusion in itself adds power and meaning to the event. At the same time, advertising and promotion have used the same music to sell their wares. Arrow's *Hot, Hot, Hot* (1984), for example, one of the most popular soca songs, has been used by Pizza Hut in their TV advertising campaign, while Bob Marley has been appropriated to advertise the Ford Sierra, Malibu, and Right Guard.

Hebdige suggests of reggae that its form resists definition, and that at least in part it is autonomous. Since 'language abdicates to body talk, belief, and intuition',[66] it becomes carnivalesque and resists containment. Jungle, with its abandonment of lyrics in favour of rhythm, might also be said to centre its meaning-making in the physical responses of its audience, the individual and communal body – a location that is hard to commodify. It is perhaps in the sound systems that one finds cultural forms that exist in the most complex relationship with mass culture. While contemporary musical forms exist absolutely as commodities within a culture industry, their consumption denies ideology in favour of jouissance. In this moment the act of being at carnival is neither compliant to hegemony, nor critical of it, but exists outside such notions. Here, then, is carnival at its most paradoxical.

A Conclusion of Sorts

Carnival by its very nature resists conclusions, for conclusions in academic discourses are as much a constructed mediation of carnival as are news summaries or promotional metaphors. Thus, despite the general thrust of this essay, I am uneasy about concluding that the carnival is contained and toothless. Certainly, aspects of its identity have been reformulated by non-carnival agencies: however, carnival is not a unitary phenomenon but heteroglossic and 'hostile to all that is immortalized and complete'.[67]

I propose that the carnival operates within a number of discourses. On one level there is the procession of *mas* and steel bands. This manifestation of carnival at its most spectacular – and in its closest association with the Trinidad heritage of carnival – is the level which most clearly speaks of cultural display and pride, but least clearly speaks of opposition or subversion. Equally, it is this particular element that, for those very reasons, is most suitable for commercial involvement. The sound systems are more clearly linked to contemporary counter-cultural and youth positions, but like all such manifestations they exist within a complex dialogue with mass culture. As noted above, their meanings are neither transparent nor cohesive.

Secondly there is the political discourse of the carnival, as articulated in the debates that surround the event both internally and externally, and as exemplified in news coverage, discussion programmes, policy statements made by the organizers, and so on. On this level the carnival becomes a focus for issues of representation and identity. Cohen and Pryce have both illustrated that the carnival is not only contested from without, but also provides a forum for debate about ideological and cultural strategies within the originating community. The very heated discussion centring on the cultural ownership of the carnival in *The Devil's Advocate*[68] is evidence enough of the seriousness with which it is taken, and of the many voices and ideological positions which comprise it. The various perspectives create an event that cannot easily be accounted for as a victim of cultural hegemony but one that is shifting, contingent upon historical circumstance and the social position of the participant.

Finally there is the commodified carnival: the carnival as site and subject of commercial exchange and promotional culture. This is made manifest in the competent organizational structure, the financial and logistical demands of the event, and the intrusion of carnival into product promotion and *vice versa*. This aspect is evidenced on the individual as well as the corporate level, for carnival becomes the market-place for a vast number of small traders selling anything that may be loosely associated with carnival pleasures. Popular culture and mass culture have an ambivalent and mutually dependent relationship with each other which is exemplified in the Notting Hill Carnival, much as the complex exchange between high and low culture was articulated within the carnival of the early modern period.

The very fact that all these Notting Hill Carnivals exist alongside each other emphasizes its dialogic composition, privileging none of the voices other than by the selective attention of the observer. Stallybrass and White warn of the dangers of essentializing carnival,[69] a process which the sponsorship arrangement, the promotional use of carnival images, and the news coverage tends towards; but by the same token it seems equally problematic to assert that these shadows of carnival are likely ever fully to contain it.

In the public eye, the carnival may now be perceived to be more socially responsible – a position that, publicly at least, the present chair of the carnival has been aiming for. On the other hand, the developments have done nothing to stop the internal debates about the position of black culture in millennial Britain, and have perhaps added fuel to the fire. As history has shown, carnival is 'poised between compliance and subversion',[70] and that is still the case with the brand-named Notting Hill Carnival. The mass youth attendance, excessive behaviour, music originating in oppositional subcultures (albeit mediated by mass culture) – all these index its carnivalesque and even subversive potential. However, mediating processes are clearly constructing an identity for the carnival which orients its operation toward harmonious, participatory, commodified pleasures, and effective reintegration. So: what's new with carnival?

Notes and References

1. Commercial sponsors have provided funding for individual elements of the carnival in the past, and the Arts Council of Great Britain (now of England) has supported the event as a whole, but it seems that these are qualitatively and quantitatively different from a commercial titled sponsorship of the whole event.

2. From a poster outside the carnival headquarters, quoted in *The Times*, 31 August 1976.

3. See John Clarke, 'Style', in *Resistance through Rituals*, ed. Stuart Hall and Tony Jefferson (London: Routledge, 1993), p. 175–91; and Mark Gottdeiner, 'Hegemony and Mass Culture: a Semiotic Approach', *American Journal of Sociology*, XC, No. 5 (1985), p. 979–1001.

4. For example, John Fiske, *Understanding Popular Culture* (London: Unwin Hyman, 1989).

5. There was in fact a small local celebration based upon a more traditionally English model in existence in the area prior to this date; however, 1966 was when the carnival as we know it today took embryonic form.

6. Abner Cohen, *Masquerade Politics: Explorations in the Structure of Urban Cultural Movements* (Oxford: Berg, 1993), p. 13.

7. Large, static PA systems, located in the side streets around the processional route and playing a variety of musical styles. Individual sound systems will often have a specific repertoire and sometimes a loyal following. They are largely based on Jamaican traditions.

8. For a full analysis, see Everton Pryce, 'Culture from Below: Politics, Resistance, and Leadership in the Notting Hill Gate Carnival: 1976–1978', in *Black Politics in Britain*, ed. Harry Goulbourne (Aldershot; Vermont: Avebury, 1990), p. 130–48.

9. Robert Hewison, *The Heritage Industry* (London: Methuen, 1990), p. 136.

10. Claire Holder, interview with the author, London, 25 May 1996.

11. Pryce, op. cit., p. 132.

12. In the main, information regarding the history of the carnival has been drawn from Abner Cohen, *Masquerade Politics,* op. cit., to which the reader is referred. See also Pryce, op. cit., and *The Road Make to Walk on Carnival Day* (London: Race Today Collective, 1977).

13. Cohen, op. cit., p 4.

14. There have of course been examples of moderately didactic *mas* presentation, but these constitute the exception rather than the rule.

15. Patricia Alleyne-Dettmers, 'Ancestral Voices: Trevini – a Case of Meta-Masking in the Notting Hill Carnival', *The Journal of Material Culture*, III, No. 2 (1998), p. 202

16. Bernard Beckerman, 'Spectacle in Theatre', *Theatre Survey*, XXV (May 1984), p. 1–13. Beckerman uses the example of a hero returning to a city (p. 6). The display that may accompany the entrance (fireworks, music, etc.) may not in itself be meaningful until associated with the deeds of the hero and the welcome of their return; and the more wonder that is generated by the pyrotechnic spectacle surrounding the parade, the more wonder is invested in the hero.

17. Holder, op. cit.

18. The Mangrove Restaurant was a cultural centre for West Indians in the area and was the spiritual home of the carnival.

19. Kwesi Owusu, 'Notting Hill Carnival', *Storms of the Heart*, ed. Kwesi Owusu (London: Camden Press, 1988), p. 239–52.

20. Will Hobson and Bill Tuckey, *The Touch Guide to the Notting Hill Carnival 1996* (London: Touch Magazine in association with *Time Out*, 1996).

21. I should qualify this, in so far as the meanings of many of these *mas* themes are not obvious to those outside the carnival community; they evoke rather than describe their meanings, and even so are not transparent.

22. Alleyne-Dettmers, op. cit., p. 205.

23. Ibid.

24. Victor Turner, *Dramas, Fields, and, Metaphors* (Ithaca; London: Cornell University Press, 1974), p, 37–42. Turner proposes that social drama is constituted by a four-stage process: breach, crisis, redressive action, reincorporation.

25. Umberto Eco, 'Frames of Comic Freedom', in *Carnival*, ed. Eco, Ivanov, and Rector (The Hague: Mouton, 1984), p. 7.

26. Holder, op. cit.

27. Richard Schechner, *The Future of Ritual: Writings on Culture and Performance* (New York; London: Routledge, 1993), p. 46.

28. Race Today Collective, op. cit., p. 9.

29. Peter Stallybrass and Allon White, *The Politics and Poetics of Transgression* (London: Methuen, 1986).

30. Interestingly, in the mid 'nineties London witnessed a number of 'street parties' generated from an entirely political perspective; these parties forced road closures in order to reclaim control of daily lives from the market system and to challenge the environmentally suspect emphasis on road use.

31. *Communitas* and structure are terms used by Victor Turner in *The Ritual Process* (London: Routledge, 1969), p. 94–130. The former refers to the spontaneous, of-the-moment, and shifting sense of community or shared experience developed within such events, and the structure is the organizing principle of the wider social context.

32. Holder, op. cit.

33. Baz Kershaw, *The Politics of Performance* (London; New York: Routledge, 1992), p. 21, where the author proposes that 'to have any hope of changing its audience a performer must somehow connect with that audience's ideology'.

34. Quoted in Julia Llewellyn Smith, 'Facing the Music', *The Times*, 27 August 1993, p. 13.

35. Herbert Marcuse, *One-Dimensional Man* (London: Routledge, 1964), p. 1.

36. Quoted in Smith, op. cit.

37. Cecil Gutzmore, 'The Notting Hill Carnival', *Marxism Today*, August 1982, p. 31–3.

38. 'It was a controversial move which split the governing bodies and carnival aficionados. Calls of selling out and fears that "wi t'ing" was being signed away were intense.' See Dianne Regisford, 'Carnival Stylee', in the e-zine YUSH Ponline, I, No. 7 http://www.leevalley.co.uk/yush/rewind/yush0107/carnival.htm.

39. Kershaw, op. cit., p. 73.

40. There have been plans to include Hyde Park in the processional route, but the organizers deny any intention of wholly relocating the carnival there.

41. David Chaney, *Fictions of Collective Life* (London; New York: Routledge, 1993), p. 19.

42. The deliciously ironic connotations of Virgin are equally at odds with the carnal pleasures of carnival, although in this case the company did not request a named sponsorship.

43. See Michael McMillan, 'The Carnival', in *Live Art*, ed. Robert Ayres and David Butler (Sunderland: AN Publications, 1991), p. 28–32., 35; Pryce, op. cit.; and Alleyne-Detmers, op. cit., p. 208.

44. Furthermore, Branson – or to be more accurate, our perception of Branson – embodies similar tensions to those operating in carnival. His balancing act is to sustain an image (and substance) of caring capitalism, to make enterprise look responsible, fun, and almost charitable. Branson, who once published the Sex Pistols infamous 'God Save the Queen' on his Virgin record label, has more recently been involved in more mainstream projects at the heart of the new-look Britain. Like the carnival, his history seems to have been one of reconciling idealism and even radicalism within a capitalist, commodity, and image-oriented context. Virgin Atlantic's sponsorship of the carnival may have lasted only one year, but in some ways the partnership seems quite apt.

45. M. Elizabeth Blair, 'Commercialization of the Rap Music Youth Subculture', *Journal of Popular Culture*, XXVII, No. 3 (1993), p. 21–34; Clark, op. cit.; Gottdeiner, op. cit.

46. During the time of the Lilt sponsorship, a number of television advertising campaigns made use of carnival imagery. In the main these were for alcoholic and non-alcoholic drinks and for a make of car. Generally the advertisements suggested that the product would turn the consumer's life into a carnival. Another example of the use of festive events in promotion could be seen in some of the Christmas lights in Regent Street in 1998, which read: ' 'Tis the season to get Tango'd', promoting another carbonated fruit drink, and perhaps gently alluding to the close relationship that Coca-Cola has maintained with Christmas imagery.

47. Robert Stam, 'Mikhail Bakhtin and Left Cultural Critique', in *Postmodernism and its Discontents,* ed. Ann Kaplan (New York and London: Verso, 1998), p. 137.

48. Andrew Wernik, *Promotional Culture: Advertising, Ideology, and Symbolic Expression* (London: Sage Publications, 1991), p. 35.

49. Ibid., p. 23.

50. Steve Pope, 'Hague's Carnival Caper Makes Us Blacks Feel Sick', *The Guardian*, 27 August 1997, p. 17.

51. Emmanuel Le Roy Ladurie, trans. Mary Feeney, *Carnival in Romans* (New York: Brazillier, 1979), p. 190.

52. Louise Downes, 'Windlashed Carnival Warms Spirits', *The Guardian*, 31 August 1992, p. 5.

53. Wernick, op. cit., p. 188.

54. McMillan, op. cit., p. 30.

55. Ibid.

56. *The Times*, 28 August 1989, p. 1.

57. The full list of such articles from *The Times* is far too long for inclusion. However, the following provides a fair indication of the trend: 30 August 1976, p. 2; 31 August 1976, p. 1, 2; 1 September 1976, p. 1, 12; 30 August 1982, p. 1; 31 August 1982, p. 2; 1 September 1982, p. 3, 9; 1 September 1987, p. 1; 2 September 1987, p. 1, 10, 11; 20 August 1989, p. 4; 29 August 1989, p. 1; 17 August 1992, p. 8; 1 September 1992, p. 1; 2 September 1992, p. 5.

58. It is notable that until 1975, when there was one article and one photograph, *The Times* remained silent about the carnival. However, in 1976 there were thirty-nine separate pieces, sixty in 1977, and forty-eight in 1988. The coverage is fullest in the year after any violent confrontation, and the overwhelming majority of these articles, written before the event, report on how the organizers and the police are convinced that the situation will be better in the forthcoming event.

59. Steve Nelson, 'Walt Disney's EPCOT and the World Fair Performance Tradition', *The Drama Review,* XXX (1986), p. 106–46.

60. Pryce, op. cit.

61. Ibid., p. 146.

62. For example, see the discussions in Blair, op. cit.; Tricia Rose, *Black Noise: Rap Music and Black Culture in Contemporary America* (Hanover, New Hampshire: Weslyan, 1993), p. 17; Sarah Thornton, 'Moral Panic: the Media and British Rave Culture', in *Microphone Fiends*, ed. Andrew Ross and Tricia Rose (London; New York: Routledge, 1993), p. 176–92.

63. McMillan, op. cit., p. 32.

64. Hobson, op. cit., p. 54.

65. For a more developed illustration, see John Street, *Rebel Rock: the Politics of Popular Music* (Oxford: Basil Blackwell, 1986), p. 219–21.

66. Dick Hebdige, 'Reggae, Rastas, and Rudies', in *Resistance Through Rituals*, ed. Stuart Hall and Tony Jefferson (London: Routledge, 1993), p. 147.

67. Mikhail Bakhtin, trans. Helen Iswolsky, *Rabelais and His World* (Cambridge: MIT Press, 1968), p. 109.

68. *The Devil's Advocate,* Folio Productions for Channel Four, produced by Charles Thompson, 6 Sept. 1995.

69. Stallybrass, op. cit., p. 15.

70. Cohen, op. cit., p. 130.

Deborah Saivetz

'What Counts is the Landscape': the Making of Pino DiBuduo's 'Invisible Cities'

In October 1998 the Italian director Pino DiBuduo visited the Newark, New Jersey, campus of Rutgers University on the occasion of the major international conference, 'Arts Transforming the Urban Environment'. For the occasion, he transformed a bleakly concrete teaching block on the Newark campus into a site for the latest of his *Invisible Cities* projects. These had originated in his Teatro Potlach company's residency in the Italian village of Fara Sabina in 1991, where DiBuduo's intention – as in a number of site-specific variations on *Invisible Cities* since – was to render 'visible' aspects of the everyday urban environment which we no longer have the imagination or the patience to 'see'. While Deborah Saivetz looks also at this original Italian project, and at a later version in Klagenfurt, Austria, she concentrates here on the Newark production, whose development she recorded – in this opening article in her own and DiBuduo's words, and in the following piece through the experiences and recollections of the participants. Deborah Saivetz holds a doctorate in Performance Studies from Northwestern University, and is currently Assistant Professor of Theater in the Department of Visual and Performing Arts at the Newark campus of Rutgers University. Her directorial work includes productions for the New Jersey Shakespeare Festival, the Drama League of New York's Directors' Project, New York's Alchemy Courthouse Theater, and the Parallax Theater Company in Chicago. She has also worked with JoAnne Akalaitis as assistant director on John Ford's *'Tis Pity She's a Whore* at Chicago's Goodman Theatre, and created original theatre pieces with Chicago's Industrial Theater and Oxygen Jukebox.

> Cities, like dreams, are made of desires and fears, even if the thread of their discourse is secret, their rules are absurd, their perspectives deceitful, and everything conceals something else.
> Italo Calvino, *Invisible Cities*

PINO DiBUDUO is the artistic director of the Italian theatre company, Teatro Potlach, based in the village of Fara Sabina located just outside Rome. Trained as a cultural anthropologist, DiBuduo has produced and directed more than twenty theatre productions since founding his company in the mid-1970s. Beginning in 1990, DiBuduo has been creating multi-disciplinary performance pieces which combine the talents of visual artists, architects, musicians, stage designers, playwrights, directors, and actors. These site-specific projects have sought to investigate the urban or semi-urban environments of European cities such as Fara Sabina, Italy; Klagenfurt, Austria; Liverpool, England; and San Angelo, Valetta, on the island of Malta. The performances collectively form a major work-in-progress entitled *Invisible Cities* which has received acclaim from both international theatre and art world audiences.

In addition to touring extensively throughout Europe and Latin America, DiBuduo has conducted numerous teaching workshops, one of which took place in 1993 on the Newark, New Jersey, campus of Rutgers University. Five years later, in October 1998, DiBuduo returned to Newark to create yet another incarnation of *Invisible Cities*. His collaborators on the project were the Austrian dramaturg Andreas Staudinger; Teatro Potlach actor Ivan Tanteri; Antonello Antonante, the co-ordinator of the Italian Centro RAT; the German journalist and television director Regine Heydeke; and the students of Rutgers University and the New Jersey Institute of Technology.

The performance was a featured event at a major international conference entitled 'Arts Transforming the Urban Environment', which brought together innovators from cultural, educational, community, governmental, and corporate organizations to explore ways in which the arts enhance the social and economic viability of cities. Lacking both the rehearsal time and financial resources he is accustomed to working with in Europe, DiBuduo envisioned the Newark *Invisible Cities* as a 'miniature' which would none the less embody the aesthetic goal of his continuing project – to *make visible* an environment which we somehow take for granted, an environment which has become so familiar to us that we are no longer able to see it.

This essay documents the rehearsal and performance process of DiBuduo's *Invisible Cities* on the Newark campus of Rutgers University. It also charts my personal journey as 'production chronicler' and DiBuduo's assistant into and out of *Invisible Cities* as I attempted to interact with and make sense of the art work before me.

September 1991
Fara Sabina, Italy

So we had more than thirty unusual rooms at our disposal, and we made them visible with our gestures, our acrobatics, our pictures, just like Marco Polo, not knowing the language of Kublai Khan, told him about the cities of the Chinese empire.

Pino DiBuduo

The interdisciplinary theatre project known as *Invisible Cities* was born in 1991 in the Italian town of Fara Sabina. This small, medieval town, more than a thousand years old, has a population of three hundred which grows to two thousand each summer. In 1976, DiBuduo and his experimental company Teatro Potlach came to live and work in Fara Sabina. The municipal government graciously offered them the use of an old monastery located on the highest point of the city to house their theatre, office, and laboratory.

Early in 1991, DiBuduo flew to Brazil to choose the South American participants for a project he was preparing. To aid him in his search for the project's theme, he brought along a number of his favourite books, including Italo Calvino's novel *Invisible Cities*. As DiBuduo drifted into a state of half-sleep on the plane, two images became superimposed in his mind. The first was a bird's-eye view of Fara Sabina with, as he describes it, its 'streets like branches, the cellars, courtyards, and squares like islands among the branches'. The second image was of the structure of *Invisible Cities,* which DiBuduo envisioned as 'cities like short stories; islands furrowed by the short dialogues between Kublai Khan and Marco Polo. Dialogues like delicate trails to overcome the empty spaces between the cities.'

As DiBuduo imagined both a geographic and narrative city viewed from above, the theme for his future project began to take shape. He would create 'a journey into invisible cities' that would begin in Fara Sabina and travel to various other cities until finally arriving in the archipelago that is Venice, 'the city in which all other cities are included' (Guarino, p. 15).

To accompany him on his search for the first 'invisible city', DiBuduo invited more than one hundred and fifty of his artist friends from all over the world to Fara Sabina. Painters, scenographers, playwrights, directors, actors, composers, musicians, and professors came from the local community itself, the surrounding province and region, and further afield from Rome, Germany, Austria, Denmark, Uzbekistan, Mexico, and Brazil. The participants were an assortment of professionals, amateurs, students, and folkloric groups such as a forty-two-person choir from Fara Sabina. Of particular importance to the development of the project, which took place over a period of one year, were a number of architects from the Unversity of Rome. DiBuduo emphasizes that 'the logic of the project is not to make a melting pot. Each artist remains with his own identity.'

The fact that Fara Sabina is almost empty for most of the year meant that numerous cellars, courtyards, and gardens were available for the company to use as performance spaces. By literally offering DiBuduo the keys to their homes, the residents of Fara Sabina played a crucial role in the performance event. DiBuduo also asked each family of Fara Sabina to contribute three photographs from the beginning of the century.

The production team superimposed fragments of text from Calvino's *Invisible Cities* onto the photographs, and then projected them as eight by four metre images onto the exterior walls of the principal church in the town's central plaza. One of the images portrayed a 1920s family posing for their portrait in the exact location where the slides were now being projected. The plaza had barely changed over the years. According to DiBuduo, 'When the traveller arrives in a new city, he may discover a past that he didn't know he had. The people went to *Invisible Cities* to recognize themselves.'

It took eleven days of work, from early morning until late at night, to make the invisible cities of Fara Sabina visible. As the artist-participants constructed their individual 'cities' with props, costumes, lights, and music, DiBuduo and his team of architects set about transforming the streets of Fara Sabina into a single, enormous performance space. Over a huge skeleton of white rope, strung in a zig-zag pattern high above the town, they laid kilometres of translucent fabric. This 'gigantic web of white clouds' functioned as a kind of road map for the spectators (or, as DiBuduo prefers to call them, 'travellers'), indicating the route they were to follow through the invisible cities.

The First Performance

Like most medieval cities, Fara Sabina is surrounded by walls and a number of gated entrance-ways. The audience was instructed to meet outside the main gates of the city for the start of the performance. The artist-participants gathered in a plaza just inside the gates, at arm's length from the spectators. The performance began as an actress wearing a clown's nose invited the audience to begin their journey into the *Invisible Cities*. The people entered the gates and followed the artists uphill along a little street to a second plaza, a path which DiBuduo describes as 'the spine of Fara Sabina'. One by one, the artists vanished into their cities, leaving only the aerial web of white fabric as an indication of the performance. The audience was thus left to search for the cities, just as we do as travellers on a journey.

Among the cities the audience would discover were an actress from the north of Italy in a cellar once reserved for animals; a group of Mexicans enacting a wake with candles, guitar music, and tequila; and four playwrights and a blindfold woman in a ground-floor library which had belonged to the first man DiBuduo met when he arrived in Fara Sabina. Now deceased, this German architect and lover of classical music had helped the members of Teatro Potlach to develop a positive relationship with the local community.

Yet another city was constructed on a hill directly opposite Fara Sabina, on which sit the remains of a fourteenth-century abbey. Once renowned for a library which attracted scholars from all of Europe, the abbey now lies completely in ruins. There are no streets that lead there, no running water, no electricity: it is truly an invisible city. On the night of the performance, eight architects built a huge bonfire inside the ancient ruins. While the architects remained 'invisible' behind the abbey's thirty metre high walls, the audience saw the illuminated abbey made strangely 'visible' for the first time.

For Fausto Bonfanti, director of the Italian company Agora Coopertivo, the most significant aspect of the *Invisible Cities* project was that it brought together an artistically, culturally, socially, ethnically, and geographically diverse group of people, yet honoured the uniqueness and autonomy of each individual. Perhaps, Bonfanti suggests, we have such a dread of the new that we are not even able to dream any more, 'for fear of discovering the invisible in ourselves'. In Fara Sabina, however, there was a noticeable absence of egoism and competitiveness. In its place was a true spirit of community among the participants, a sense of 'forging a new way together' (Guarino, p. 39).

June 1992
Klagenfurt, Austria

Three months before assembling the participants for his second *Invisible Cities* project in Klagenfurt, Di Buduo travelled to the site with his production team and dramatic advisor, who toured the site in an attempt to discover in Klagenfurt 'the equivalent of the inner spaces of Fara Sabina' (Guarino, p. 92). Klagenfurt is located near a beautiful lake with waters so clear that every year, on 5 May, the local residents drink a glass of lake water to demonstrate that it is safe for tourists.

Interestingly, DiBuduo felt drawn not to the historic town centre, as he had originally imagined, but to this lake, its surrounding woods, and the Lend Canal, which had been built to transport water after the town had suffered two damaging fires. At the far end of the lake, the team discovered the picturesque castle and chapel of Maria Loretto, which they envisioned as the destination of a long voyage.

Di Buduo was intrigued by the fact that this spectacular lake remained 'outside the field of vision' for the present-day citizens of Klagenfurt, who visited it only for the occasional Sunday afternoon picnic or romantic retreat. He imagined the canal and the old photographs he discovered in the town's museums and private homes as lifelines – one spatial, the other temporal – to this forgotten layer of Klagenfurt's history.

One of the more remarkable photographs that DiBuduo came across portrayed a misshapen dwarf holding a bottle under his arm. According to local legend, a dissolute city once existed on the land that is now the lake. On three occasions, the dwarf advised the people of the city to mend their ways. When they failed to heed his third warning, the dwarf removed the stopper from his bottle and and the city became engulfed by water. After the depraved city disappeared, the present city of Klagenfurt was built further away from 'the scene of the crime'.

To make the submerged city 'visible' once again, the *Invisible Cities* team constructed a floating barge which seemed to emerge from the lake to the heavenly strains of a full Corinthian choir. At the same time, the present-day lake and canal were rendered 'invisible' by expanses of white fabric laid over the surface of the water. The very same material that had facilitated travel for the audiences of Fara Sabina was now used in Klagenfurt to inhibit passage on the canal. As the audience crossed the bridge over the lake, they were unable to see the familiar sight of water. Arriving on the other side, however, they saw the water's reflection on the white fabric. The audience, while prevented from seeing the water in its everyday guise, was thus given the opportunity to view it in from an entirely new perspective.

Finally, DiBuduo wanted to make 'visible' (in the sense of creating access to) a scenic area on the lake's shore that was normally off-limits to the public. In order to visit this lovely but privately owned spot during the performance, the audience would have to cross a five hundred meter span of water at a point far from the lake's only existing bridge. When DiBuduo approached the municipal governent of Klagenfurt with the idea of building a second bridge, the town officials replied, 'No problem. We'll call the army.' The army completed the bridge in two days. As DiBuduo explains, 'Every year they must do exercises.'

Klagenfurt, the birthplace of the authors Robert Musil and Ingeborg Bachmann, is a cradle of Austrian literature. As the audience journeyed through the woods surrounding the lake, they saw fragments of these writers' texts and old photographs and sketches of their city projected onto various surfaces – the white fabric covering the water, the trees, the ground, and a helium balloon launched at the start of the performance to make the sky above Klagenfurt 'visible'.

After three preliminary production meetings during the year leading up to the project, the 175 artist-participants constructed the Klagenfurt installation of *Invisible Cities* in just twelve days. By concealing the obvious and revealing the hidden, DiBuduo discovered the 'invisible cities' of Klagenfurt and made them appear anew.

October 1999
Newark, New Jersey:
a Production Chronicle

Marco Polo describes a bridge, stone by stone.
    'But what is the stone that supports the bridge?' Kublai Khan asks.
    'The bridge is not supported by one stone or another,' Marco answers, 'but by the line of the arch that they form.'
    Kublai Khan remains silent, reflecting. Then he adds, 'Why do you speak to me of the stones? It is only the arch that matters to me.'
    Polo answers: 'Without stones there is no arch.'
                             Italo Calvino, *Invisible Cities*

A few weeks before DiBuduo's scheduled arrival in Newark, the following audition notice is posted around the campus of this large, urban commuter school, situated in one of America's cities most in need of revitalization: 'Looking for students interested in visual arts, architecture, lighting design, sound design, graphic arts, music, circus performance, dancing, singing, acting, and any other creative talents.' A large number of students sign up for interviews with the director, a process they hope will be less intimidating than auditions.

They are eager to work with and learn from an internationally renowned artist whose way of making theatre is supposedly unlike anything they have experienced. They are also intrigued by the idea of transforming familiar campus locations through the medium of performance. Meanwhile, the frustratingly convoluted business of securing permission from the University to rehearse and perform in 'alternative spaces' has been set in motion – a process which will continue right up until opening night.

9 September: the Director Appears

After introducing himself to the crowd of interested students who have gathered to be interviewed, DiBuduo explains the history and purpose of *Invisible Cities*. He informs us that the project has always involved an international gathering of artists who work in relation to a specific environment, and whose purpose is to transform that environment in such a way that those who normally take no notice of it will suddenly perceive it anew.

Each actor involved in the project builds his/her own 'city', which exists independently of yet is connected with all of the other 'cities'. The actors are responsible for constructing their cities out of architectural and scenographic materials such as wood, fabric, stage props, costumes, lights, and sound, as well as for choreographing a sequence of actions with a beginning, middle, and end, which they will perform repeatedly over the course of the performance. According to DiBuduo: 'A city can be a dream, a business, or a solution to a problem, but always at its centre is the human being struggling with his identity, community, and relationship to society.'

DiBuduo proceeds to outline our work process. Our first step will be to choose a space within the University. We will then work each day building our cities, with the goal of 'making the invisible visible'. Finally, we will find a way to connect the individual cities. DiBuduo explains that his usual way of working is to begin each rehearsal with a meeting to discuss technical problems, after which the participants go off to their own spaces to develop their cities. They have another meeting at lunchtime, then spend the afternoon working once again on their cities: 'It's just like building a city.'

DiBuduo cautions us that *Invisible Cities* will not involve 'acting' as we know it, nor is it about 'somebody coming and doing their own installation'. Rather, its purpose is to discover a relationship with the space itself and with the memory of that space, and to build bridges among the different people participating in the project. DiBuduo advises us that, throughout the process, we must patiently observe and listen to the space. In this manner, 'the performance will arise'.

DiBuduo remarks that – by contrast with Italy, where 'everything is beautiful' – the campus 'doesn't give pleasure. Everything is cement, artificial. It is not a town.' However, despite his disenchantment with the physical environment, he is eager to familiarize himself with the histories, myths, and legends of the individual students. He announces that

Pino DiBuduo, with the author (left) and a visiting journalist at the 'Arts Transforming the Urban Environment' conference, Rutgers University, 1998. Photo: Melissa Zachariades.

we will begin our next meeting by presenting ourselves, and invites those who speak other languages, paint, sing, dance, or play musical instruments to demonstrate their talents. He asks all the student to bring in their favourite family photographs – the older, the better – and two songs from the past twenty to thirty years, one of which is from their own ethnic background.

The students are also requested to read Calvino's *Invisible Cities* and prepare three passages of text which in some way capture their imagination. DiBudo ends the meeting by reminding us that, 'We are all on the same ship', adding: 'This is not a performance, it is another way to proceed.' I wonder whether he is referring to the upcoming 'presentations' or to the *Invisible Cities* project itself.

10 September: the Auditions

DiBuduo conducts his interviews, or 'presentations' as he calls them, asking each would-be participant questions such as, 'Can you present a fragment of your work?', 'Can you do something for me?', 'Can you make a fragment of a dance?' The students' offerings include a *t'ai chi* demonstration, a tap-dance routine, a booming song from the musical *Jesus Christ Superstar,* a sacred hymn sung in Latin, a recitation of original poetry, a nostalgic song in the Tagalog language about the loss of independence in the Phillipines. One student timidly confesses to DiBuduo, 'Basically, I dance. Any other talents I have are undiscovered', and I realize that there are 'invisible cities' within each one of us, waiting to be excavated.

A young woman shows off her double-jointedness and converses with DiBuduo in Italian. A visual arts student of Puerto Rican heritage shows DiBuduo graphic designs, slides of his original art work, and some family photographs. As DiBuduo carefully examines the old photographs, the student begins to relax. I sense a personal chemistry between them as they laugh and exchange words in Spanish. It strikes me that DiBuduo is indeed the anthropologist trying to find a way into this strange, young culture which inhabits a physical environment that, at least for the director himself, offers little aesthetic charm. Making theatre, discovering 'invisible cities' around and within us, is DiBuduo's way of entering into a relationship with the culture that is Rutgers–Newark.

Confused about the purpose of the interviews, someone asks, 'Are we *auditioning* for you?' DiBuduo replies that he has not come to Rutgers to judge the quality of the students' talents and skills. Rather, he is conducting these interviews in order to discover a context, a point of departure for the project. He recognizes that both the rehearsal process and the resulting performance of this particular *Invisible Cities* may differ significantly from his previous projects in Europe. He explains: 'Today's interviews are a starting point, a way for me to get to know you better. To learn, for example, that a student named Cara Mia does not look, nor speak a word of, Italian. I don't know why I'm going in this way but I listen and react. One thing is certain: it is not direct.'

At first, I assume DiBuduo's last statement refers to the nature of the creative process, specifically his own process. I later realize that he has also described, perhaps unintentionally, the peculiar actor–audience relationship that characterizes *Invisible Cities*. He proposes an example: 'You are playing the piano. Not like in a show, but as if you are in your room. Then you begin to speak a poem. But as if you were alone in the room.' DiBuduo's illustration seems to suggest that the *Invisible Cities* participants will engage in a series of actions that is to be less a *performance* of behaviour for the benefit of the audience than behaviour enacted, in an almost 'private' way, for themselves alone.

When the presentations are completed, DiBuduo informs the actors that all of them will be included in the project. He then shows photographs from his *Invisible Cities* projects in Fara Sabina and Klagenfurt, pointing out that, because the arts in Italy are subsidized by the state, he has the freedom to make theatre that is not commercial. Explaining that the raw materials of *Invisible Cities* are (1) the People; (2) the Space; and (3) the Ideas (which include Text and Memory), he adds: 'I've been looking at the space, I've met the people, I know the texts.'

From these elements, DiBuduo informs us, he will fashion the Newark version of *Invisible Cities*, arriving not at a presentation but rather a simplification of his continuing project. The next step will be to explore potential performance sites on campus, discovering how to make them at once 'visible' and 'invisible.'

14 September: Administrative Frustrations

DiBuduo holds a brief production meeting with members of the technical theatre staff, who have spent the past several weeks – months even – attempting to secure permission for DiBuduo and his crew to wrap campus buildings in huge expanses of fabric; send actors rappelling off rooftops; light fireworks displays; and hang lighting instruments and actors in trees. The adminstration refuses to give definite answers, preferring to give various reasons why DiBuduo's scenographic proposals are sure to fail: there is no rooftop on campus strong enough to support even a single person; we must not occupy academic buildings until after nine o'clock, when evening classes let out; in order to proceed with the project we must take out an additional (and prohibitively expensive) insurance policy; and so on. We are in a holding pattern, uncertain whether *Invisible Cities* will be given permission to exist.

22 September: Selecting the Site

After spending a week at an arts festival in the north of Italy, DiBuduo returns to Newark with his European collaborators. He meets the actors and technical staff in the campus quadrangle (or 'piazza,' as he prefers to call it), the first stop on their search for possible performance sites. The company then proceeds to Hill Hall, a characterless concrete building whose enormous central ramp gives it the appearance of a parking garage.

Interestingly, DiBuduo sees possibilities in this building. He leads the group up and down the ramp, describing a vast array of images: the priest Marco Polo sitting on a chair suspended from a wall; Kublai Khan hanging from a harness attached to a high beam; the end of a hallway draped with black scrim fabric to create a Victorian bedroom; an actress lying on a flower-strewn bed here; an actor working at a computer terminal there. DiBuduo has found what he has been searching for. He christens Hill Hall the site of *Invisible Cities*. The process of re-visioning the space has officially begun.

25 September: Building the Cities

DiBuduo assembles the actors in Hill Hall and instructs them to 'find' their space. They are to begin building their city and choreographing the sequence of actions they will perform while inside it. By the end of today's rehearsal they must present DiBuduo with a list of whatever set-pieces, props, costumes, lights, and 'manpower' they will need from the technical staff. DiBuduo travels through Hill Hall, surveying each city and responding to the work-in-progress of its creator. Through a series of questions and answers, suggestions and improvisations, the director and actors begin to co-imagine their cities.

One of the actresses seeks out a cavelike space under a concrete ramp that, she confesses, she has 'always wanted to go in'. She crouches in the space for nearly two hours, trying to imagine her city from DiBuduo's point of view while the director himself consults with other actors and the technical staff. The actress, feeling a bit abandoned, is drifting off to sleep when she suddenly becomes aware that DiBuduo is staring at her. He asks how she feels being in the space. Regaining her composure, she replies that she feels as if she is in a cave.

DiBuduo proceeds to drape a cloth over the actress's head, suggesting that she is from Greece. He informs her that she will be washing her hands in a transparent basin filled with blood, and asks her what else she would like to have in her city. She replies that she would like candles and some type of ground covering. Both actress and director like the idea of covering the floor of the city with straw, but the technical director vetoes the combination of candles and straw for safety reasons. Later, I ask the actress if she *feels* like an actor in rehearsals. 'Not really', she answers. 'Not yet. I feel like a wait-er.' She admits that she has been tempted to do her homework while waiting her turn to interact with the director, but is not sure 'if it's okay'.

Another actress, mystified by DiBuduo's way of working, is struggling to understand what is expected of her. Unable to remain alone in her as yet unformed city for any length of time, she wanders through the building seeking direction and the company of her fellow actors. When I ask her questions pertaining to her city, her persona, or her sequence of actions she is completely at a loss. DiBuduo has given her a number of suggestions but she seems unable to make them real for herself.

A third actress walks around Hill Hall for about half an hour, investigating a number of possible sites. Eventually, at the end of a hallway, she discovers a space enclosed on three sides by large plate-glass windows. She sits in the space for a while, and begins to imagine herself as a bird who can see the outside world but cannot escape from her glass cage. As the actress contemplates the natural world outside the windows, as well as her own past, her city gradually takes shape in her imagination:

My city came about through my fascination with the world beyond the windows. Not only did I want to create a city inside Hill Hall that was nature-like, I also wanted my ancestral past to be a part of it. The person I am today is, in large part, influenced by my family and my ancestors. I began to think about what I represented, who my family was, and what my ancestors did on

Kublai Khan (Daniel Pagan) in his harness, from Pino DiBuduo's production of *Invisible Cities*, Rutgers University, 1998. Photo: Melissa Zachariades.

their land in Portugal. In my city, I portrayed my great-grandmother, a widow, surrounded by her vineyard in Portugal. I created my city thinking about the details of her life, my family's tradition of winemaking, and nature. In addition to the actual grapevines I brought from my own backyard in Newark, I envisioned fog in the air and red light shining upon my body which would be covered with black clothes. I asked the technicians to drape the walls with black scrim fabric in order to block the light spilling into my space. The rest of my set design was influenced by Pino. He suggested focusing a green light on the grapevines to enhance the colour of the leaves, and very specific background music – the Portuguese group Madre Deus's score from the film *Lisbon* – which created the exact mood I was trying to achieve.

28 September: Singing in Unison

DiBuduo leads the actors through a series of warm-up exercises – literally 'conducting' them as they recite fragments of memorized texts and sing childhood favourites such as 'Itsy Bitsy Spider', 'Rock-a-bye Baby', 'The Hokey Pokey', and the Spanish song 'Cielito Lindo'. The actors must speak or sing in perfect unison while responding vocally and physically to DiBuduo's hand movements as he signals changes in pitch, volume, and emotional intensity. I suspect that even these exercises are an integral part of DiBuduo's vision of theatre-as-construction-project, in that he is using them to develop the flexibility and responsiveness of the actors as his 'raw materials'.

I wonder, does this have anything to do with acting? Observing somewhat regretfully that the intended effect of the exercises seems to be training the actors to respond almost instantaneously to DiBuduo's direction, I also notice that a sense of ensemble, of *esprit de corps*, is deepening among the cast members. For this reason alone, I conclude that the exercises serve an important purpose and do in fact have quite a bit to do with acting.

28–30 September: Technical Troubles

DiBuduo calls a production meeting with the technical staff. Visibly upset, he explains that he is trying to 'find the University logic', trying to understand how to work, trying to find the chain of command among the technical staff, because he is confused about who to go to when he needs something. He and the actors have 'found certain cities in Hill Hall' and he must know when they will be able to work with props. He cannnot even depend upon his stage managers, who fail to show up consistently to rehearsals. He must have the technical director with him at all times; otherwise, it is impossible for him to create the performance. DiBuduo is also frustrated that many of the students have not cleared their schedules in order to be free to rehearse each day from four o'clock in the afternoon until midnight. At the close of each rehearsal, he must know which students will come the next day.

The University bureaucracy is only making matters worse. Because Hill Hall is an academic building, where classes meet all through the day and evening, the actors and technicians are forced to strike all of the cities after each rehearsal and construct them from scratch the next day. The fact that we have no storage space in the building, and must transport all of our equipment from across the campus, doubles the set-up and break-down time. DiBuduo argues, understandably, that we must be able to store everything needed for the construction of the cities in a secure room inside the building. The technical director tells DiBuduo that he does not know if this will be possible, whereupon DiBuduo explodes: 'How is it possible to manage if the University doesn't know? I cannot work in this way, with this logic. We must find a way to work together.'

DiBuduo ends the meeting by reassuring the technical staff that he doesn't want to judge, he simply wants to know: 'I am not so strict. I will find a way to oblige you. I just need to know.' Two days later, he presents the technical staff with the following list of props:

1. Fireworks.

2. Mountaineering ropes and harnesses for the actors who will be rappelling and hanging.

3. Helium gas for inflating balloons.

4. Candles to be used in the finale (The technical director suggests using outdoor lawn torches, but

Motaz Diab (top) and Ann Kirolas and Rodney Reyes (kneeling), being coached by dramaturg Andreas Staudinger, in two of the *Invisible Cities* from the Rutgers production. Photos: Melissa Zachariades.

DiBuduo nixes the idea. 'People are used to that kind of thing here', he explains. 'We have to make a landscape that is more unusual.')

5. Strings of tiny light bulbs and Chinese lanterns.
6. A real bed.

Our technical director takes DiBuduo outside to the 'piazza' and describes a special effect he has devised for the opening of the show, complete with fog, glitter, red light, and jazz musicians playing their instruments while perched in the trees. He asks DiBuduo, 'When the piazza turns red, would you like to see the library go red, too?' DiBuduo replies, 'No, because you can put a lot of light there and it won't change anything. No, in my logic. No, in your logic also. It will take too much time.'

The technical staff then begin discussing the process by which they plan to superimpose Calvino's text on all the students' family photographs, just as they did in Fara Sabina. Strangely, DiBuduo rejects the idea, saying: 'No, that is not necessary. If we do that the audience will look at the text and not the image. The image is what's important.' Laughing, he adds: 'We need to control what the audience is seeing at every moment.' While I understand that DiBuduo has been feeling 'technically challenged' since the project began, I am somewhat taken aback by his headstrong reaction. I cannot help but wonder if his desire for absolute control extends beyond the audience's perception of the stage image to the theatre artists with whom he is supposedly collaborating.

Inside Hill Hall, DiBuduo has rigged a rope and harness from one of the concrete crossbeams. He is helping an actress into the harness, encouraging her to execute aerial backbends and somersaults while singing hymns in Latin. Students rush through the performance space on their way to and from classes, staring at the tutu-clad actress dangling high above their heads. An elderly man in a suit wants to know, 'What's going on here?' and disappears without waiting for an answer. A female administrator asks, 'Can we walk through here?' The university community is beginning to take notice of the altered space. The 'invisible' is being made 'visible'. And DiBuduo, the tension now gone from his face, is delighted.

1 October: Creating a 'Proposition'

I ask DiBuduo what I can do to help him, particularly with regard to his work with the actors. He replies with a sense of urgency: 'They must remain in the space, even if it is for two hours. They must make a "proposition", something they can do in the space and repeat.' He asks me if I will stay by his side at the next rehearsal, and help him to communicate with the actors.

I look up the word 'proposition' in the dictionary, fearing that I may be losing something in the translation. I discover that a 'proposition' is, among other things, 'a plan, a task'. DiBuduo is asking the actors to devise a sequence of tasks, or actions, that they will repeat in their cities over the course of the performance. Some of the actors are also having difficulty with the repetitive nature of the assignment, complaining that they feel like robots or automatons. Here DiBuduo's emphasis on 'doing', however repeatedly, is important. Acting, after all, is doing. The student actors are unaccustomed to *doing* for themselves. And even more experienced actors too frequently depend upon their directors, teachers, and coaches to inform them what they are supposed to be *doing* at any particular moment on-stage.

2 October: Revisiting the Cities

The technical director and Teatro Potlach actor, Ivan Tanteri, have spent the morning shopping for candles. Tanteri is searching for large disk-shaped candles with a thick wick. They are nowhere to be found, at least not in the greater Newark area. The technical director suggests grouping several votive candles on a plate, but Tanteri wants to keep searching for the exact candle he has in mind. The technical director, on the other hand, cannot afford to spend his valuable time hunting down the perfect candle. He explains, 'We are all involved with other things, especially our jobs. We do not live off our art.' Painfully aware that DiBuduo and his team are accustomed to working with far more time and financial resources at their disposal, he is finding it a challenge to satisfy all of the director's technical requirements, even for this 'miniature' version of *Invisible Cities*.

Later that afternoon, DiBuduo and I take a tour through Hill Hall to observe the cities-in-progress. DiBuduo confesses that the insecurity of the actors is making *him* feel insecure. We visit the cavelike city of the actress playing the Greek woman. DiBuduo reminds her that her actions must be real, definite, concrete. She must neither 'act' nor pretend, but really read, really wash her hands, really eat something 'from the tropics'. This last suggestion is surprising, given that the actress is supposed to be portraying a Greek woman, but DiBuduo has his own 'logic'. He tells her that she is 'a strong Mediterranean woman like Judith, who can kill her husband even though she loves him because she is the Queen'.

We proceed to the city of the actor playing Marco Polo. DiBuduo and the actor, now costumed as a priest, decide that the city should be filled with water, 'like Venice', an idea which turns out to be technically impossible. DiBuduo has another idea, though: the actor will sit in a chair attached to the wall. The image is both visually and psychologically provocative, yet not much more feasible from a technical standpoint. We approach the city of the suspended ballerina. She is hanging in her harness, practising her acrobatics and sacred music. She asks to have a stool in her city so that she may rest if she needs to, but DiBuduo says: 'No. You must continue singing and dancing for the entire performance.'

Finally, we come upon the actress who has been unable even to begin creating her city. DiBuduo presents her with a bunch of plastic flowers, leads her to a narrow walkway overlooking an atrium surrounded by classrooms, and tells her she is on a bridge waiting for her husband to return from being out at sea. I suspect, however, that this actress requires something more concrete to work with, something that will really activate her emotionally. Privately, I suggest to DiBuduo that perhaps she is pregnant. 'Okay', he says. 'Tell her. She is pregnant.'

The majority of the actors find the freedom they have been granted to develop their own cities both challenging and inspiring. Others are confused and need (or think they need) more direction. They have difficulty incorporating the seemingly arbitrary adjustments that DiBuduo suggests when he visits them each day in their cities. They don't quite understand what is expected of them, yet are timid about approaching the director with their questions. And they are perplexed by the fact that while DiBuduo meticulously shapes their external, physical sequence of actions, they are left on their own to create their inner, emotional journey.

3 October: Refining the Cities

At the meeting that launches each day's rehearsals, DiBuduo continues to ask the actors what they need for their cities. An actress approaches him, saying: 'I need a veil. And I showed you the wedding dress but you didn't like it.' DiBuduo replies, 'I never say, "I don't like it." I say, "It doesn't work." Because this is not a theatre. This is a space.' He reminds the actors that they must continue to perfect their sequence of actions. It is not important whether the sequence lasts thirty seconds or three minutes, but they must show him something that is precise. I now understand that a 'proposition' is, in fact, a 'suggestion'. The actors 'suggest' a sequence of choreography, a prop or a costume piece to DiBuduo who responds by either approving the actor's 'suggestion' or proposing an alternative.

I ask DiBuduo if there is anything in particular he would like me to discuss with the actors as we observe their work in the cities. He replies, 'It is not really a matter of speaking to them, but of controlling them. They must stay in their space and focus on their actions. They must not act but do. They must *perceive the space*. If I go over to an actor and say, 'That is good', then they will start 'acting' and it will become artificial. They must build and take responsibility for their space.'

Two students approach DiBuduo with their idea of constructing a Spanish colonial house on the roof of Hill Hall, which the spectators will view from inside the large glass windows. But DiBuduo dissuades them from this idea, saying: 'You are acting, but we cannot feel the *reality of it* because you are separated from us by glass. And this glass is not even clear, it is [tinted] brown. So we lose a great deal of your physical presence.' We visit the actress playing the Greek woman eating tropical fruit in her cave. DiBuduo suggests that she is now a gypsy.

5 October: Unifying the Space

The technical staff have rigged one of DiBuduo's large white cloths on the Hill Hall ramp in such a way that it masks much of the sterile ugliness of the building. The fabric seems to unify and enclose the space, creating a strange, almost womb-like feeling. It changes everything. The following images run through my mind: the Wrapped University . . . the Rapt University . . . the Men of the Cloth. I tell them to DiBuduo who jots them down in his notebook

7 October: Notes to the Actors

As we are about to begin the final dress rehearsal, DiBuduo addresses the actors, who have gathered around him in a circle:

This is something that takes time. You must take the time, and not be always, 'Tatata tatata, oh yes, oh yes, oh yes.' [He mimes running around at a frantic pace.] *When you take time to listen, you help the nervousness inside. If you are silent for one minute, you will begin to feel one minute of your life. Not one year, but one minute. You will feel how much there is inside of you for two minutes. You must decide to be silent. Because when you do, time will become very long and the space will change.*

We have a lot to do here today. That is why I was so angry before that we could not practise. The spectator will come here the same as each one of you, full of thinking, full of pressure, with an objective. There is always an objective. If you are here for one moment, you must do something.

I am here to change that. To change, meaning to make visible *changes. To make more time, more space, more things. But if, from the beginning, I don't practice, I don't know how much time the spectator will need to change and to watch. I repeat,* to watch. *I want the spectators to watch, because they arrive all full. As if they are going to the theatre. They sit like this: 'Let's go.'* [He mimes a spectator sitting and clapping his hands as if to say, 'Let's get this show on the road.'] *I don't like all this. I want to introduce them to something else, to put them in a different condition.*

Remember, no one is to speak with any of the spectators. Don't change what you are doing. If there are no spectators, don't leave your city. You must continue your logic even if you don't see anybody. Because if you are in your city, and people are there watching another city, you are still in the space, you are still creating the space. Be patient, you will see. Because we are creating this together, from the beginning. You remember that day the technicians wanted to make decisions, but I couldn't commit to the space the way it was? The space made you lose energy all the time, it was confusing. Now it's more concentrated, the spine is right there. [He points to a vertical pole in the centre of the space.] *It's all in the spine, you see? Without this construction, the building cannot exist. Without the spine, you cannot stand up. It's all energy.*

When Antonello comes to your city, you will all exit in the same direction. Follow Antonello outside and go do the cloth. People who have music in their city must turn it off before going away. Slowly, not in the rhythm of everyday life. Antonello comes, you count one–two–three–four–five seconds, you turn off the music, then you prepare what you must do to leave your city. Somebody must come with the ladder for Rafael. Somebody must help Dej get down from the harness. We must organize this tomorrow. It must be clear. We cannot call for somebody's help during the performance.

Tomorrow afternoon we must practise. We must organize where you will find the torches when you go outside and where you will put the torches before going inside. Be careful when you are under the drapes. You must go always in a line, don't cut the space, follow the first person. And go close to the big building, not too close but close enough. And look with open eyes at the flame of the torch. Not directly, but the flame must be within your 180 degree vision.

Is it possible to practice outside tomorrow at five o'clock? Immediately after, you go build your city, even if there are people here. You practise what you are to do, prepare yourself there, repeat your script, your action. This means that all the cities, all the lights, everything must be finished at seven-thirty. Then you go to change. Take your time, you have one hour. Don't speak too much among you. Try to remain light, but in relationship to the work that we are going to do. It doesn't mean that you cannot speak at all, but try to avoid speaking about last summer or. . . . At eight forty-five, you must be ready, with nothing more to do. At nine o'clock we must begin.

Remember the process. We are building the process now. We are forming the process. This space is another space. When we take it away the day after the performance, they will miss it. But they will see it is possible to create the space. Because we did it together. It is possible to make something together.

8 October: Opening Night

The audience of students, faculty and Urban Arts Conference attendees who have been sitting for the past half-hour in the campus student centre are growing restless. *Invisible Cities* has been scheduled as an official conference event, and DiBuduo plans to introduce the performance with a lecture and slide show. But it is almost nine-twenty. Finally, the director appears, looking a bit frazzled. He proceeds to instruct the audience in the history of the *Invisible Cities*, informing them that tonight they are about to have an experience similar to that of the spectators in Fara Sabina.

He explains that this particular *Invisible Cities* will be only 'a fragment' because he is working with only fifteen students as opposed to the two hundred or so participants to which he is accustomed. Moreover, the space itself is a fragment. Normally the performance occupies a combined interior and exterior space ten to twelve times the size of Hill Hall. 'But, as an exact fragment', he adds, 'you will have, in the moment, the exact experience.' Then, like a hybrid of mad scientist and Pied Piper, he leads the audience into Hill Hall to experience *Invisible Cities* for themselves.

8 October: Notes to the Actors, Part Two

When the performance is over, DiBuduo once again addresses the actors:

I saw you all in your situations, in this position, with this behaviour. I was so happy because something has happened that we could only make happen together. Really fantastic. Ah, que bello. To see all your faces. Really, it was good work from each one of you.'

He tells the actors that tonight he had to 'understand the logic and define the timing', because he hadn't been able to rehearse enough, especially the finale. For this reason, he didn't see much of their work, but tomorrow he will spend more time in the cities:

Tomorrow we will do the same work. Prepare very well. Don't think that tomorrow you know everything. Tomorrow is the first day. And the day after tomorrow will be the first day. Every night is the first night. Because there is always the possibility to reach someone through the theatre. We will meet here tomorrow at five o'clock, so we can prepare and fix things. There are many details. The first thing we will do at five o'clock is a little meeting to define how the time will go. Then we will start immediately to build the cities. We will repeat some practice because outside, of course, we couldn't prepare. Okay? Thank you very much.

Performance as the Story of Space

Theatre is a continual erasing of the tracks in its own landscape.

Fabrizio Crisafulli

Fabrizio Crisafulli, professor at the Academy of Art in Catania, Italy, and a participant in the Fara Sabina project, has suggested that *Invisible Cities* is not about the preparation and staging of a play, but rather about 'the coming together itself in a certain place, in order to hear what this place ha[s] to say in

63

our presence'. Acknowledging that the basic idea of theatre is usually tied to the idea of 'doing,' Crisafulli suggests that the essential dimension of DiBuduo's work may have more to do with 'not-doing', and that a new condition of the actor might be the ability to be present in the here-and-now (Guarino, p. 60).

I would argue, however, that the ability to exist on-stage 'in the moment' is hardly a new idea, particularly for actors trained in the methods of Stanislavsky and his artistic progeny. It is an ability that any actor worth his or her salt must either possess naturally or cultivate. Moreover, to be able simply to be present in the here-and-now, while an admirable quality in life, is not enough in the theatre. An actor must not only *be* but also *do* authentically: otherwise there is no drama.

Over the years, DiBuduo's *Invisible Cities* project has brought together visual artists, architects, writers, and theatre people from a variety of cultural backgrounds. While all theatre entails the coming together of a group of artists in a specific place in order to tell a story to a particular community, the 'spine' of DiBuduo's site-specific theatre is neither the dramatic text (although the piece incorporates images and textual fragments from Calvino's novel) nor the inner life of the actor. The motor that drives DiBuduo's imagination, the central axis around which *Invisible Cities* turns, is place.

The story of the performance is the story of the place. The actors respond less to each other than to the place. The audience leaves the performance reflecting upon the nature of place. Scenographic elements such as fabric, furniture, props, costumes, lights, and sound draw our attention far less to the performers *in* the space than to the space itself, which has been transformed into both dramatic protagonist and leading actor.

DiBuduo believes that we all too quickly lose our capacity to perceive what lies hidden in our everyday surroundings. We are no longer able to see what initially surprised us in the cities in which we live and work. His mission is thus to discover what is hidden and make it reappear so that we may see anew. Just as Marco Polo conjured the various cities of his world travels through story-telling in order to make them 'visible' for Kublai Khan, DiBuduo and the student actors of Rutgers–Newark invoked, and evoked, their cities through the medium of performance. Like ambulatory 'readers', the spectators moved through Hill Hall at their own pace, each interpreting the cities through their own senses and imaginations.

One Rutger–Newark student confessed that at first she did not understand the concept of *Invisible Cities*. As she worked with DiBuduo and the other student artists, however, she slowly began to formulate her own concept of the piece:

There are spaces we walk past every day but do not notice because they are empty or meaningless to us. By filling these space with cities, however, we come to see a once-empty space from a new perspective. The audience reflects upon and observes the space, now filled artistically and theatrically as a city. The project is called *Invisible Cities* because the performance does not normally exist in that empty, unnoticed space. But the space itself will remain even after the performance has ended.

Hill Hall has now returned to its normal, ugly self, yet phantom memories of *Invisible Cities* remain. While we can easily numb ourselves to the concrete, *visible* presence of our surroundings, the absence of the *invisible* – not only what we did to the building, but what we went through together – insists upon making itself felt. It is engraved in our experience, reminding us that there is a great deal more to life than what can be seen. The extraordinary theatre-making skills of DiBuduo demonstrated that the visionary thinking of the Urban Arts Conference could be put into practice. *Invisible Cities* revitalized a campus. It, and we, will never be the same.

Note

Unless otherwise indicated, all quotes attributed to Pino DiBuduo are drawn from the author's rehearsal notes for *Invisible Cities*, directed by DiBuduo, Rutgers University, Newark, New Jersey, September–October 1998, as well as from informal conversations with the director.

Sources

Italo Calvino, trans. William Weaver, *Invisible Cities* (New York: Harcourt-Harvest, 1972).
Raimondo Guarino and Andreas Staudinger, *Città Invisibili* (Austria: Alekto Verlag, 1993).

Deborah Saivetz

'Every Light Form Has a Shadow': Acting in 'Invisible Cities'

In the foregoing article Deborah Saivetz described the background to the creation of Pino DiBuduo's *Invisible Cities* on the Newark, New Jersey, campus of Rutgers University in October 1998, and the development, limitations and strengths of that production. Its 'audience' – for the most part members of the university community and attendees at the concurrently scheduled 'Arts Transforming the Urban Environment' conference – were impressed by DiBuduo's artistic vision and the conviction of the actors, though a few expressed disappointment that, despite the project's urban setting and conference tie-in, *Invisible Cities* seemed to have little to do with the historically and culturally rich city of Newark itself. Most, however, were fascinated by, and perhaps even grateful to, the visiting Italian director who, with his band of student artists, transformed an ordinary campus building into an at times baffling, frequently delightful, and always provocative sequence of worlds – as if, as one witness put it, 'watching a dream in real life'. The actors and technicians who participated in *Invisible Cities* confronted challenges from all angles: the English–Italian language barrier, the University bureaucracy, the physical limitations of the performance space, inclement weather, and the shortage of finances, human resources – and, most of all, time. Yet, despite the constant 'changes of direction' that were part of the *Invisible Cities* process, the actors were inspired by DiBuduo's willingness to allow them complete artistic licence in the conception and execution of their cities, and they came to understand that even artistic tensions can strengthen the bonds within an ensemble, infusing its members with a fighting spirit that refuses to let the project die. In the following interview, the student artists reflect upon the unique process of creating *Invisible Cities,* the actor–director relationship, the role of the audience, and the effect of the project upon the Rutgers–Newark community.

The normal performance provokes analysis, the performance-event provokes confession.
Georges Banu

WHAT WAS UNIQUE *for you about working on* Invisible Cities?

Rodney Most of the productions that I've seen or worked on start out with a basic story – a text. Then the director chooses the space. On this project, Pino began with an idea which wasn't fleshed out *until* he chose the space. When they arrived in the space, Pino and the actors talked about what the space might look like to them, what it might look like to the audience, and how the actor would like to create the space.

Daniel The project was created in such a short time. I've never had to rehearse so intensely before. In terms of creative expression, we worked without a set script and Pino let us invent things. That was very interesting.

Did you have a greater degree of artistic freedom than when working on a more conventional play?

Daniel A lot more, but with that freedom came more responsibility. We were all responsible for finding our own props, costumes, and developing our own city. You couldn't go overboard creating your city or you'd spend all day setting it up and breaking it down.

Lillian I think what was unique about *Invisible Cities* was learning about all the restrictions and the adminstrative 'red tape' behind the project itself. For example, we still hadn't been given permission to hang the big, white drapes off the buildings when we began rehearsing. There were a lot of restrictions involved, it wasn't just like, 'Oh, let me take this fabric, or let me use this light.' You had to go through a whole chain of people to get what you needed. That was something I had never even thought about.

As performers, you were exposed, in a much more immediate way, to the technical aspects of making theatre. And often you had to deal with the technical side of things yourself rather than rely upon the director.

Rafael Performing in Hill Hall was a unique experience. I had never done an environmental piece before. A theatre stage is a very secure and comfortable space. Performing in a space where anything and everything could happen was a bit overwhelming.

Lillian There were a lot of distractions going on. People were going to and from their classes, and would walk through the performance space while we were setting up and getting into character. I felt as if I kept going in and out of focus, and had to work twice as hard to stay in character and not let the surrounding environment affect me.

Joe For me, the unique thing about this project was the actor–audience relationship. In most other productions, you go on-stage and you look out into the black room where you can't really see the audience and can hardly hear them. In this performance, the audience was interacting with you. Some of them would try to talk to me, and several times I'd hear people say, 'I can't hear you. Speak louder.' Part of you wants to accommodate them, but at the same time you have to stay in character. Some of the actors had horror stories about audience members taunting them. Adrian [*the actor who played the priest Marco Polo*], for example, was called 'the devil' several times. It was a bizarre feeling, because the audience was not stationary, but were moving through the space, viewing you from different angles, and interacting with you on different levels. *You* were stationary.

How did the audience's responses affect your performance?

Joe Sometimes I got thrown off. It required a lot of concentration just to stay in character. On opening night, I was lying down with my arms stretched out at the beginning of the performance, and I had to keep from laughing because an audience member said, 'I think he's dead now.' I had to tell myself to ignore that. The audience is experiencing your performance and the whole space in a very different way. They're going to react in very different ways, and a lot of them will verbalize that reaction by asking you questions or trying to get a response from you. They want you to acknowledge that they're there.

Maria I actually liked that part about the performance. I did get annoyed quite a few times, but the fact that the piece demanded a lot more concentration from us as actors was our challenge. I tested myself with it. I'm sure that many of the students here at Rutgers had never seen a performance like *Invisible Cities*. It was new for us and it was new for them. I knew that they were uncomfortable, but it didn't bother me because I felt so secure in my spot. I was in my own world and felt fine being there.

Adrian I felt very insecure in my spot. Someone from the technical staff told me to be careful and watch out for anyone who might have a blade or a knife. And during the first performance I was a little shaky because someone was pulling on my robe. They were trying to see what I was wearing underneath, and how I was hanging from the wall. They were very curious but, at the same time, they were invading my space.

Were you able somehow to channel your insecurity as a performer into the character of the priest?

Adrian Yes, that affected my character. I found that I could turn my body a bit and

Adrian Hernández as Marco Polo, in Pino DiBuduo's *Invisible Cities* at Rutgers University, 1998.

interact with the audience. Sometimes I even scared the audience away. During the first performance, I heard certain audience members comment that I wasn't speaking loudly enough. That affected me and for the next performance I was louder. Someone also commented that I was crying and needed tissues, when I was actually sweating.

Daniel I would watch Adrian from my city. Both of us were very vulnerable because we were supported by harnesses. I'd get kind of scared when the audience would enter the building because they'd see me first. There would be a wall of people coming right at me. They'd step on my tarp and want to steal my rocks and want to touch my leaves. That's all right, that's fine. But then they'd want to come close to *me*. I was a little more fortunate than Adrian in that I was able to swing around on my harness and could sort of keep the audience at bay. I'd swing up and down, so that I could look at each one of them and they'd know, 'Okay, that's his space, that's the distance he needs.' Adrian, on the other hand, had such limited mobility. He was tilted at an angle and could only twist a little from side to side. It's very difficult to perform when people are constantly poking you and asking questions.

Lillian Especially when you're not supposed to interact with them.

Daniel Exactly. You *can't* interact.

That was the rule?

Daniel Yes, we could speak but we were not supposed to interact. Sometimes, the audience would try to make us laugh. They were trying to 'kill' Adrian; it was so horrible. I was fortunate enough that, if I were to laugh, I could just hang upside down and talk to myself.

Did you feel like an actor? Or did this dynamic between you and the audience make you feel more like a museum exhibit or a creature in a zoo?

Rodney Ann and I had audience on three sides of our city, and they were constantly moving in a kind of traffic pattern from city to city. We also had people who were actually sitting down and watching, which was great because usually when you're onstage you can't really see the audience. Ann and I weren't really making eye contact with the audience, but sometimes people were right behind me and I could hear them breathing, speaking, and even taunting. At least they were responding, whereas in a theatre you often can't tell. It shouldn't affect your performance, but I was glad to know in the back of my mind that people were interested in what was going on in my city and the other cities around me.

Rafael I felt both secure and insecure in my city. Secure in the sense that I didn't have the audience around me because my city was so high off the ground. And because I didn't have much direct contact with the audience, I was able to concentrate. At the same time, I felt insecure because I was up so high, my space was tiny, and I was doing a lot of dance movements. One false step and I could have fallen ten or fifteen feet to the ground.

Joe I felt more fortunate than some of the other actors because they were completely exposed, whereas we had a scrim in front of our city. Nobody violated that scrim. It was like a fourth wall that protected us. On the night of our last performance, though, I was tempted to open up the scrim and pull somebody into my city.

I suppose it depends upon your temperament, both as a person and as an actor, as to how much you want to feel that sense of protection.

Maria The sense of ensemble was different, too. We were all working on our own cities and were very far apart from each other physically. That was difficult. We did keep sneaking out of our cities to see what the other actors were doing. I thought that was interesting.

One day in rehearsal, Pino led the actors around the space to see all the other cities. Did this help to give you a sense of the piece as a whole?

Lillian Ribeiro – 'like a caged bird' in Pino DiBuduo's *Invisible Cities*. Photo: Melissa Zachariades.

Joe You saw the other spaces but not the performances *in* those spaces. During rehearsals for a more conventional play, you often have the chance to sit in the audience and watch the way the other actors are reacting to that one particular space. On this project, I was able to see a lot of what Daniel and Dej were doing because they were in my line of vision. I didn't have a real understanding, though, of how the space was affecting the other actors or how they were affecting the space.

How did you develop your individual cities?

Lillian At one of our first rehearsals, Pino said to us, 'Walk through the building, find your space and create your city.' As I began to walk through Hill Hall, I felt drawn to a space surrounded by windows that was very far off from everyone else. I sat there for a while and thought, 'Well, what am I going to create? What is my city going to be about?' I took out my journal and I started writing whatever came to me. I wrote about how I felt like a caged bird that could see what was outside, but couldn't escape. I just kept writing and asking myself, 'How do I want to reach the audience? What do I want to tell them?' I knew that I wanted to tell them who I am, what I'm about, where I come from, and that this had to do with my family background and tradition. I wanted to tell them, 'I'm from Portugal. This is what my family used to be about. This is my great-grandmother in her city.' That's how I discovered my city – I wanted to tell the story of my ancestors, my tradition, my country. Then I started asking myself what kind of mood I wanted to create, and began to think about lighting and fog. I knew I wanted music but I wasn't sure what kind. Pino suggested that I use the music of the Portuguese group Madredeus, and I'm so glad he did. That was the biggest influence that Pino had on my city. The music did so much for me: it helped me discover who my characer was and what I wanted to tell the audience. And it had such an enormous effect on the audience. It really drew them into the mood of my city.

Did the music activate you emotionally?

Lillian Yes. Especially because we had to repeat our sequence of actions so often. Being enclosed in such a small space made me feel almost compelled to repeat the same things over and over. At the same time, you don't *want* to do the same things over and over, because you know that the same people are watching and you want to keep entertaining them as well as yourself. It feels almost psychotic in that you're doing the same thing, staying in the same space, looking at the same thing yet the music somehow makes you feel more lonely, more happy, more angry. The music affected everything I did.

One of the challenges in this type of work is, as you say, 'to keep entertaining yourself', to stay engaged as an actor when you're limited by the space, the text, and your actions which you must keep repeating. . . .

Rodney Originally I didn't have a city. I was a stage manager for the production. But during the last week of rehearsals, we had a meeting with Pino and he told me, 'Rodney, we will create a city for you. It will not take too long. We will take three days to work it out. Something easy for you. Maybe we will put you on a computer.' The next day he was working with Ann who was originally supposed to be a suspended mermaid. And while Pino was working with her, I heard a lot of laughter. I wondered what was going on, so I pulled the drape aside and walked into her city. I saw Pino on the bed tickling Ann. She was laughing and I thought, 'Oh, that's interesting.' Pino turned to look at me and said, 'You. Come here, come here. Do this, do this.' So I began tickling her and Pino directed me to get up on the bed and start playing with her. I found myself thinking, 'Oh, I guess I'm in this scene.' The next day I was driving and had an idea for the city. When I told Pino my idea, he said, 'No, no, no. I see you talking with all these women during the rehearsals. That is who you are and we will put that in the city.'

Adrian My city was developed for me. It was very simple. My costume and my rosary were my city.

Did you choose anything on your own? Did you say, 'I want to be in this space', or, 'I want to be a priest'?

Adrian No. Pino chose me to be Marco Polo, the priest. Most of us didn't know that Marco Polo *was* a priest. Even the audience was surprised to learn that he was a priest.

How did you feel when you were told that you would be hanging from a harness attached to a high beam?

Adrian It didn't bother me. I started out as an architecture student and I like to set limits for myself. Having a lot of freedom to move around in my space would have driven me crazy. I needed someone to put me in my place.

Dej Pino asked me whether I was afraid of hanging, and I said, 'No.' A few days later he tried a harness on me, and asked me to try doing dance-like movements while hanging upside down. He said, 'Don't be afraid, just lean all the way back.' I did and felt really comfortable. I was an angel, and was happy with my character and my space. I wasn't exactly greeting the audience because they visited other cities before mine, but I did greet them with happiness. I sang songs in Latin, and the words were, 'Praise the Lord.' The songs were upbeat and happy.

Maria My city was sort of developed for me, too. My space originally belonged to another actress but she had to drop out of the project, so I said, 'Fine, no problem. I'll use that space.' We just changed the context of what was happening in that city. It became more of an emotional kind of city. It wasn't as extravagant as some of the other cities which had a lot of technical elements. My city took about two minutes to set up.

Who chose your costume, the flowers that covered the floor of your city, the slides that were projected on your pregnant belly?

Maria The costume was the only one available and probably the only one that would have fitted me. The flowers had already been laid out in the space, but in a different way. At first, I was supposed to be on a bed or chair, but Pino suggested that I sit on the floor. The slides were going to be projected on the wall with some kind of coloured spotlight on me. Pino just decided one evening to project the slides on me instead. And then I chose the slides that I liked.

What about the texts you spoke in your cities? Did Pino choose them?

Adrian Pino chose my text from Calvino's *Invisible Cities,* but I changed it because I didn't want to be repeating exactly what Daniel was saying. I didn't think it was appropriate even though Pino suggested that we were having a conversation in front of the audience.

So the conversation never happened?

Daniel Actually, Pino saw it and said, 'No, don't talk to each other.' He separated us and developed something else.

Rafael My city went through a number of changes. I chose my space because it felt isolated and I wanted to work with that feeling. When Pino first saw the space, he came up with the idea of me being a sailor stranded on an island. It went from that to being a small child in his own little world, to being an insomniac, to being a groom whose bride had died on the day of his wedding, to being a waiter who aspired to be a matador.

Did these changes come from you or from Pino?

Rafael For the most part they came from Pino. My greatest challenge was dealing with all of those changes. I became very frustrated and angry. But finally I was able to work through that. Pino always told us that we needed to be 'in the moment'. He'd say, 'Don't think about it. Do it.' As I was setting up my city and draping my chair for our final dress rehearsal, the idea for the matador just came to me. Pino actually liked it. He said, 'That was very good because you were being precise.' And then, at the very last moment, right before the opening performance, he added a table to my city. That's how the waiter idea came about.

Daniel Pino had originally wanted some of the actors to be up in the trees and I volunteered. When we weren't able to perform in the trees, I chose to hang inside Hill Hall. In terms of my props, both Pino and I would suggest things. Most of the props in my city were my own stuff that I brought in. Pino wanted the Calvino text written on the tarp that covered the floor of my city. He asked me to speak that particular text as well. At first I didn't like it because it was one story repeated over and over and over and over. I felt very uncomfortable with it until I saw that it intrigued the audience. Then I kind of grew to like it. I would repeat the same thing over and over, and the audience would stop and actually try to listen to what I was saying. At first, it didn't seem to make any sense to them, but it forced them to stop and try to understand what I was saying.

Did the audience affect you in a positive way?

Daniel It depended on individual audience members. Some people came only because it was a class requirement. They needed to understand what was happening, so they'd ask me, 'What are you doing?' I'd look at them and just speak my text. I'd try to make them understand, 'Marco Polo described a bridge.' And then there were the Urban Arts Conference people who were very interested in what was happening. They'd stand and watch you and really try to appreciate what was happening. And there were others walking around saying things like, 'This is stupid. What the hell is this?' But even so, I could tell that they were interested. I, too, liked the fact that they felt uncomfortable, because it meant that the performance stirred some emotion in them. And you try to work with that. You see they're uncomfortable and you try to make them comfortable. We weren't supposed to interact but, in a way, we could. I could look at them and speak to them, but it was more as a story-teller than a feeling of 'I acknowledge that you're there.' I was acknowledging the *story* of Marco Polo.

Did Pino direct you not to acknowledge the audience?

Daniel He specifically told us, 'Don't talk to the audience. If they speak to you, don't speak back to them. Just do what you're doing. You mustn't acknowledge that a specific individual is there.' But I had to address the audience as a whole. To do this, I had constantly to flip around in my harness.

Directors often talk with actors about motivation or objectives. Did you miss not being given much psychological or emotional direction? Or did you feel relief at being liberated from all of that?

Rafael I really did miss that. I also missed not having a text to say. Pino wants everything to come from the actor. He really doesn't want to tell the actor what to do. He wants the actor to find it himself.

It seems that Pino wants the actor to generate his or her own inner *life. On the other hand, he is quite specific about directing the actor's physical behaviour. He knows exactly what he wants to see imagistically.*

Rafael As I mentioned before, Pino would say, 'Don't improvise. Just do it. Don't think about it.' And I found that very frustrating, because how am I supposed to *do* something if I don't know *why* I'm doing it. I have to think about it first. As an actor, my emotions are what propel me to action. It wasn't until the last couple of nights that I finally understood what Pino meant, and I just did it.

Did you find that 'just doing it' produced an emotion in you?

Rafael I think so. My frustration began to create certain emotions inside me. It actually gave me the energy to sustain my actions throughout the piece.

Maria My city started out as a kind of bleak-looking space. When Pino first visited my city in rehearsal, he sat in my space with me for a while. A couple of rehearsals later, he told me, 'I want you to smile.' I didn't really want to smile, but I tried it and my city changed into something else. In terms of finding the inspiration, it was all up to me. I just drew on things that have happened in my life, things about me. Sometimes you're playing a character and you have no clue how to begin. I think that's when you need direction. But when the character you're playing is you, in your space, with your emotions . . . that's pretty easy.

Did Pino's warm-ups and singing exercises make any sense to you? Did you enjoy them? Did they seem to serve any purpose? Was there a connection between the exercises and the work on the cities?

Lillian I just was thinking back to being in this rehearsal room doing those exercises. It was very strange at first. We were singing 'Itsy-Bitsy Spider' as a group. I hadn't done it in so long that I was doing it all wrong. And then we were doing the 'Hokey Pokey'. I felt very childish. I kept laughing and it was really difficult for me to concentrate. But after a while we really got into it, as adults. It also demanded real breath control.

Adrian I got frustrated with those little exercises. I ended up with migraines. But the positive thing about them was that they helped me to relax in front of everyone. They forced me to be a part of the group. I never thought I could have sung a solo in front of all those people but I did. And we learned to control our breath and make choices vocally.

Rafael The exercises helped us to find a comfort zone with each other and brought us together as a group. They also helped us to focus our breathing. In one exercise, Pino conducted us and we had to react vocally to whatever his hands were doing. We had to express the emotional quality that matched what his hands were doing.

I'd like to address the issue of 'artistic difficulties'. Conflict is, of course, an inevitable part of the creative process. To what degree did it enter into this project? Were you able to deal with any tension that arose and still create?

Dej I got angry at one point when Pino said he wanted me to hang upside down, sing, and flail my arms around 'like an animal'. I thought, 'Oh, great. I'm going to be an animal hanging upside down wearing a white dress.' And then he asked me to sing the same song over and over again. I didn't want to bore myself *and* the audience, so on the nights of the performance I sang several different songs in Latin. I changed the choreography, too, so I wouldn't hurt my back. I didn't feel a lot of tension because I just quietly decided to change things on my own.

What did you do when Pino passed by your city?

Dej I did what he had originally asked me to do.

Lillian I felt tension not so much with Pino, but with some of the technical staff and other actors.

More so than when working on other plays?

Lillian Yes. This is the first time that I have really felt tension towards a lot of other people. I had been told in my directing class, 'Okay, you're going to go be part of this project. It's your mid-term. Put together your own space. Do what you want to do. Be creative.' I would have gotten involved in the project anyway, but I probably did more because I was in the directing class at the time. So I developed my ideas, and began telling people what I needed, like, 'I need a fog machine, I need lights, I need an arbor built, I need black mesh cloth to cover the walls.' The technical staff said they didn't know whether they'd be able to get me the things I needed. I got upset because I felt as if I had been given the chance to create and all of a sudden it was being taken away from me. So I began to demand things, and if I couldn't get them from the technical staff, I went directly to Pino. And I got pretty much everything I wanted in the end.

Did that allow you to have a greater understanding of Pino's frustration when he needed things from the technical staff and couldn't get them?

Lillian Yes. A lot of the time I defended him to the other actors. I would say, 'You know, you have to understand that he's not from this country. He's used to working in a different way.' I felt really compassionate towards him. I knew he was being demanding but I also knew he wanted to get things done. All directors can be jerks at times. So what? So can we, when we don't get what we want as actors. I think we have to be understanding of someone who's trying to put a project together.

Do you feel you grew, as actors, working on this project? Are there things you can take from this experience that will affect your work on more conventional theatre projects?

Rafael This was a completely different type of performance experience for me. I had no text. I was just out there in the open. It was a challenge just to be there, working until two o'clock in the morning. We'd arrive at rehearsal at five o'clock in the afternoon and wouldn't get started until nine or ten at night because of all the technical things that had to get done. I'd be sitting in my city for hours, doing nothing. It was especially difficult for me because Pino would say, 'Go to your cities,' and I'd need a ladder to climb up to mine. Hours later I would still be stuck up there. At times, I actually caught up on my sleep while waiting in my city. Or I would have to jump down because I became stir-crazy. But in terms of growing as an actor, I discovered that, yes, I can do it. I can do a movement piece and sustain it over a period of time. I can repeat a sequence of actions, maintain the emotional quality, and not look stagnant or fake. The other thing I've learned is that, if I want to be in this business, you're going to encounter people like Pino who are very eccentric and have outrageous ideas. They may ask you to do things that you don't want to do, or think you can't, do, but you'll never know unless you try and challenge yourself.

One of the things Pino wants to do with Invisible Cities *is change the way that people perceive their everyday environment. Did he accomplish that with this project? How has* Invisible Cities *affected the Rutgers–Newark community?*

Joe I think the performance made a great impact. Many people, whether they understood the piece or not, said it was unlike anything they had ever seen before. Their reactions fell into three categories: 'I didn't get it', 'It was interesting', or 'It was great'. Pino would often say to us, 'Two minutes of your life.' And it made sense. The people who came to *Invisible Cities*, whether they appreciated it fully or not, were affected because they took 'two minutes of their life' to see something new. To see something that is possible. Something that not necessarily is, but could be.

Maria And I thought, 'Thank God for that.' Because that doesn't happen a lot here. Most of the students go to the theatre only when it is required for a class. We do such incredible things in our little theatre programme and not very many people know about us. It felt good just to get our work out there. Whether they hated it, whether they shouted at us, whether they stepped in front of my light. . . .

Rafael Another thing that this *Invisible Cities* achieved was to make Hill Hall look beautiful! It's such an ugly building. The ramps make it look like a parking garage. The people who saw *Invisible Cities* are going to remember that I was above the doors near the exit sign, Ingrid was under the ramp in a city full of hay, Dan was hanging from the rafters. That was Pino's point. You see the environment every day. You look at all the buildings on campus and everything is always the same. But after seeing *Invisible Cities,* you're going to look at Smith Hall and see five actors running back and forth with a huge white drape that's hanging from the roof.

Daniel Pino said he wanted the audience 'to miss' what they had seen. I think those who saw the show *will* miss what they saw, which was so interesting and so once-in-a-lifetime. And when they remember it, they'll think, 'Wow, that was really nice.' It really did stir something in them.

Rafael It even stirred the people who were coming in and out of classes while we were rehearsing. Many of them would come up to us, stand there staring and ask, 'What are you doing? What is this for?'

Lillian The Rutger students I know who went were completely awed by the performance. They thought the overall concept was so impressive – the way we changed the space, the way that Rafael was standing on top of the door, the way Rodney was running around the bed, the way Motaz was sitting outside under a tree smoking his pipe, the way Adrian was hanging off the roof beams. If we had had more time, maybe just one more week, and more technical support, I think we would have blown people's minds.

What does the title Invisible Cities *mean to you?*

Joe It refers to the cities within us. You are an 'invisible city', because you carry within you all of the memories, experiences, and sensations that you've encountered in your life. When you relate with another person, you recreate that life for the other person to experience along with you. It's there living inside you, but the other person can't always see it – just like the cities we created working on this project, which are fantastical and real at the same time. You can't actually see them until someone relates them to you in performance. Lillian's city, for example, exists within her because it's part of who she is, it's why Lillian is sitting here right now. That city within her came to life because she told its story in music, movement, and light. All of us had somehow to tap into a part of ourselves, express it, and materialize it. Our cities were all so different. Daniel, as Kublai Khan, says, 'It is not the stones, but the line of the arch that is important.' Each one of us is so different that the cities seem incongruent. But the line, the arch, the pattern that emerges from them, becomes the most important thing because it joins everything together. All of these strange cities collide, mesh, and become a whole world within Hill Hall. Just as we walk around with all of these different and unique 'invisible cities' inside us, but somehow we still manage to connect.

Lillian For me, *Invisible Cities* is taking hold of an open space, creating something out of it, and allowing others to observe it – as Joe said, making 'the city' within you come to life.

Rodney The invisible city is there. It has always been there. It has its own story, its emotions, scenery, and people. But you can't see it unless you bring it to life.

And the project made all of this visible?

Rodney Yes, for as long as the show was running.

Rafael Another thing that Pino would ask us was, 'What is the space doing to you?' You can create anything you want in your city. Anything can happen. It's just a matter of finding within yourself what you want to make visible for others to see.

Adrian It reminds me of taking something from nature, a flower for instance, and pulling it apart. And describing a petal so different from all the others, even though all of the petals are related.

Rodney It took a lot of effort but it all worked out in the end. Great things don't come easy. Every light form has a shadow. Without the shadow, how can you appreciate the light?

Note

The author wishes to thank Adrian Hernandez, Maria Laguna, Joseph Manese, Dej Mejia, Daniel Pagan, Angela Pereira, Sherise Pruitt, Rodney Reyes, Lillian Ribeiro, Michè le Rittenhouse, and Rafael Rodriguez for their critical comments and participation in this interview.

Sam Ukala

Impersonation in Some African Ritual and Festival Performances

Few studies of African ritual and festival performance have been written from a theatrical perspective, and Sam Ukala believes that the richness of such events has yet to be fully explored by African dramatists – while most of the western paratheatrical experiments derived from them have been influenced more by anthroplogical models than aesthetic principles. In pursuit of a dramaturgical approach to the study of African rituals and festivals, he focuses on the role and nature of impersonation in these events, and examines the relationship between the forms, objectives, and contexts of the performances and the kinds of impersonation to be found in them. Distinguishing between the western actor and the African role-player, and between 'intense impersonation' and possession, he suggests also some generic parallels between western theatre and African performance. Sam Ukala is a Professor of Drama and Theatre Arts at Edo State University, Ekpoma, Nigeria. A theatre director and playwright, his published plays include *The Slave Wife*, *The Log in Your Eye*, *Akpakaland*, *The Trails of Obiamaka Elema*, *Break a Boil*, and *Two Plays: The Placenta of Death* and *The Last Heroes*. In 1998–99 he was resident writer and director at Horse and Bamboo Theatre in the United Kingdom, where, with Bob Frith, he wrote and directed *Harvest of Ghosts*, a first experiment with wordless visual theatre, an extension of his preoccupation with 'folkism', a dramaturgy based on folk compositional and performance aesthetics formulated in his article in NTQ47 (August 1996).

IMPERSONATION in the theatre may be defined, for our purposes, as the imitation of the appearance, speech, and behaviour of a character. Intended to communicate artistic truth as faithfully as possible through the instrumentality of the actor's disguised body and voice, impersonation is the nucleus of realistic or psychological acting, but it also occurs with varying intensity in most other forms of performance. It is an aspect of mimesis, but while mimesis includes the imitation by designers and technicians of settings and other environmental factors, such as light and non-human sound, impersonation is limited to the imitation, through the actor's body and voice, of the appearance, speech and behaviour of the character in the play.

In drama, the fully delineated character has three dimensions, which Lajos Egri calls 'physiology, sociology, and psychology' (p. 36–77). Physiology refers to the character's physique, appearance, gait, and clothing; sociology to his status, occupation, and interpersonal relationships; and psychology to his mental and emotional states: intelligence quotient, reasoning faculty, complexes, motivations, drives, temperament, etc. In the playscript, the three dimensions are represented by words in the dialogue of the characters and in stage directions. In performance, they are bodied forth by means of impersonation: an actor whose physique may resemble that of the character is costumed, made-up, assumes a gait and voice, carries properties, and generally acts as is appropriate to that character.

Impersonation, therefore, is achieved through the joint efforts of the visual artists and the actor. To impersonate a king, for example, the actor does not only imitate the king's voice, gait, and behaviour, he is also invested with royal regalia and appearance by means of costume, make-up, and properties. Yet to imitate a character's psychology is to go deeper than external manifestations. '"I am impersonating someone" ends, and "If I were such and such a character, what is the nature of my feelings and [thoughts] . . . ?" begins' (Stanislavsky, p. 95).

When the actor has found the right answers to the question, feels those feelings, thinks those thoughts as truthfully as possible, and lets them determine his physical movement and behaviour on stage, his impersonation is at its most intense. He is at the brink of a precipice beyond which comes the fall into the deep and unfathomable gulf of trance, possession, and loss of self-control. At this brink, he puts himself *consciously* into the shoes of the character, with a degree of concentration capable of making him seem dead to all extraneous stimuli. Ability to remain at this brink without toppling over is the hallmark of *intense impersonation*, while the imitation through body, voice, and mind of the three dimensions of the character is *comprehensive impersonation*.

Acting in Rituals and Festivals

Role-players in African rituals and festivals cannot be rightly called actors in this current western sense. For example, they do not memorize and deliver already written lines; the roles they play are determined not by their talent and theatre training, but by their birth, status, age or vocation; they do not put on their act, which may be once a year, for money or fame, rather their performance is rooted in religion and worship. However, it provides entertainment as well as palpable social and material benefits for their communities.

We would thus call them performers, in the broadest sense of the word. According to Xerxes Mehta, 'performers are themselves, exist in real time, and perform or "do" the various tasks or activities that the piece requires. Actors impersonate others, exist in stage time, and respond to their characters' inner psychological promptings' (p. 189). Mehta warns that the difference between the performer and the actor is not absolute, since performers can 'demonstrate characters in the Brechtian fashion and sometimes also act illusionistically' (p. 189), but stresses that, unlike the impersonator, the performer is not expected to present 'a coherent personality developing consistently through time'. Rather, he 'may sketch out a social type inside an image and then vanish mid-sentence into another image' or return simply to ' "himself", doing a task in real time' (p. 190).

A performer is, therefore, not always disguised to look like a particular character, but if, according to Mehta, he sometimes acts 'illusionistically', then he sometimes impersonates and responds to the character's 'inner psychological promptings' – and, with particular reference to the African ritual or festival performer, this may be done either in real time or in stage time punctuated by real time.

Our objective here is to determine the extent of impersonation in some African ritual and festival performances. This is intended not only to make specific African performances more understandable to dramaturgs and researchers, and, perhaps, provide a clue to paratheatrical practitioners as to where to look for possible inspiration or models, but also to foster a literary critical approach to the study of African rituals and festivals, which have often been condemned as non-drama by scholars who rely mainly on anthropological studies or on models of the western well made play.

Richard Schechner notes, rightly, that 'what may be a "movement" in Europe and America is the most widespread kind of theatre and dance in many parts of Africa and Asia' (p. 150, note 18). He refers to 'performance activities' and, by extension, much of the European and American avant-garde theatre movement. But the kind of theatre and dance that he describes as 'widespread . . . in many parts of Africa' manifests in traditional rituals and festivals, the richness of which there is as yet no avant-garde theatre movement in Africa to explore.

That this is so may be attributed to three causes. Firstly, a majority of the African elite, among whom are most of the African playwrights and theatre directors, have yet to renew interest in traditional theatrical performance, which their former colonizers and educators disparaged or banned, in favour of western drama. Secondly, some African playwrights and theatre directors who could have adapted rituals and festivals to their purposes lack a working knowledge of their various elements from a theatrical perspective, studies of these being in short supply.

The third cause relates to the impact of Wole Soyinka's theatre. Soyinka, the first African Nobel laureate, is the outstanding adapter of the aesthetics of African (Yoruba) rituals and festivals to the literary drama. Several of his plays, notably *A Dance of the Forests*, *The Road*, *The Strong Breed*, *Kongi's Harvest*, and *Death and the King's Horseman*, pulsate with ritual and festival presence. His cyclical plots, sparse narrative content, large numbers of characters, largely unrealistic and unpsychological characterization, cryptic language, symbolic music, and oracular dances (sometimes by masked figures) are all borrowings from African rituals and festivals. But it is hard to guess which particular ritual or festival any of the plays is based on, for Soyinka's robust imagination often truncates and grafts festivals, uproots, transplants, and cross-breeds the essence of mythic sources, or tumbles and reverses sequences of otherwise familiar rites (see Ogunba, 1970, p. 8–10; 1971, p. 106).

This results in the complexity of much of his theatre and its consequent unpopularity with African audiences (see Adedeji, p. 140–2, 147; and Okpewo, p. 218), who cannot recognize and identify with its aesthetics. Perhaps wary of this pitfall, other African playwrights – for example, J. P. Clark, Bekederemo, Efua Sutherland, Femi Osofisan, Ama Ata Aidoo, and Sam Ukala – largely avoid adapting the aesthetics of the African ritual and festival, preferring as more comprehensible the aesthetics of the African folk-tale.[1]

It may well be that Soyinka's style is a reflection of the aesthetics of the rituals and festivals that he adapted. For the African ritual or festival is, indeed, more composite and complex than Soyinka's theatre. Thus, it combines visual art, myth, theatre, religion, magic, and life, and – unlike Soyinka's plays, has no stage directions or dialogue to clarify its plot, action, and characterization. If the current search by African scholars and playwrights for an indigenous dramatic aesthetic principle[2] is to be fruitful, more African experiments with the aesthetics of African rituals and festivals are required; but these will not be possible until African theatre practitioners thoroughly understand the various aspects of such events.

Such an understanding may best derive from studies of specific aspects of the performances. It might be useful to know, for example, how much magic there is in the make-up applied in African ritual or festival performances, and also the principles of its application – especially since it was the magical aspect of these performances which partly caused the colonialists, who could not understand them, to outlaw them or deny them recognition as theatre.[3] Here, then, I have chosen to concentrate on the aspect of impersonation: this has been an element in most theatrical performances of all ages since early man's re-enactment of a hunt or of the the reproduction process. Yet its importance to different kinds of performance has varied, and this variation has yielded different kinds of drama.

Ritual: the 'Bori' and the 'Orukoro'

We shall explore eight African ritual and festival performances, beginning with two rituals, the *bori* of the Hausa and the *orukoro* of the Kalabari. For descriptions of the *bori*, we rely on Andrew Horn's 'Ritual, Drama and the Theatrical: the Case of the Bori Spirit Mediumship' and Dapo Adelugba's 'Trance and Theatre: the Nigerian Experience'. Adelugba's essay deals also with the *orukoro*.

Both forms employ trance and possession. In his description of the *bori*, Horn tells us that the *mai bori* or *'bori* medium' is costumed in clothing reminiscent of the *iska* – that is, the 'spirit' that regularly possesses her. She also carries 'the *tsere*, a fetish, contrived from objects and clothing associated with the particular *iska*', which functions as more than a stage property, as it is 'the vehicle through which the spirit possesses the medium' (p. 190). But a devotee may function as a possessed medium or as a mere dancer possessed. As a medium, 'the *mai bori* [in her dance] will assume the demeanour of the spirit and her movements, voice, words, knowledge, and powers will be those of the *iska* "riding" her'. As a possessed dancer, she

> begins to dance, to move erratically, to jump in the air and land squarely on the buttocks with legs splayed apart, or to jerk wildly about. The spirit is now presumed to have occupied her body and, in the imagery of *bori*, she is said to be 'ridden', 'mounted' (*hawa*), by the *iska*; she becomes the mare (*godiya*) of the spirit.... There will be no fully realized characterization of the occupying spirit and the performance will simply be a display of ecstatic hysteria with a musical accompaniment (p. 190).

At the end of her ecstatic dance, observes Onwuejeogwu, the possessed

> falls exhausted and is covered with a cloth. During this state she may foretell the future. Spectators wishing to obtain a favour from or appease the spirit that has mounted her, place their gifts and alms on the mat. Then she sneezes, the spirit quits her, and she becomes normal. During this period she is never referred to as herself but as the spirit (cited in Adelugba, p. 204–5).

Now to Adelugba's description of the *orukoro*. The *orukorobo* (priest or priestess) wears the usual ceremonial dress of African priests, priestesses, and medicine men: white and red cloths, coral-bead necklaces, wristlets, anklets, and Indian bells. The *orukorobo* also carries objects for his/her work: an elephant tusk – a symbol of authority, which, like the *tsere* of the *mai bori*, may be a vehicle through which he/she is possessed; 'a saucer containing a fresh egg, some alligator pepper, and/or kolanuts and coins, which significantly are part of the sacrificial offerings' (p. 211).

While dancing, the *orukorobo* makes ritual sacrifices and incantations. As he/she becomes deeply ecstatic, he/she is 'transformed into the essence of the god. Thus a priestess who in ordinary life is known to be very effeminate, old, and weak can be transformed into a fierce, agile, bold, and awe-inspiring character, capable of commanding the worship' (p. 210). The *orukorobo* becomes 'capable of the prophet's sight, communicating with man as a first-person representative of the deity' (p. 210)

Three patterns of activity emerge from the above descriptions. Two are manifested in the *bori*: the performer consciously assumes the physiology (appearance) of the spirit, but is later imbued with the psychology (intellectual and emotional state, behaviour) of the spirit when she performs as its medium; the performer assumes the physiology of the spirit and dances until she is possessed and imbued with clairvoyance rather than the spirit's psychology. The third pattern is manifested solely in the *orukoro*, in which the performer, without assuming the god's physiology, is 'transformed into the essence of the god' with powers of clairvoyance.

Impersonation and Transformation

Two elements are common to the two patterns of activity in the *bori*: (i) conscious imitation of physiology; followed by (ii) a state of unconsciousness, in which the medium or the possessed communicates as spirit to man. The second element also occurs in the *orukoro*. Neither involves impersonation, for the impersonator has a dual personality: at every stage of his performance, he is himself, planning, executing, controlling his art, emotions, and movement; he is also the representation of a character. But in the *bori* and *orukoro*, the performer possesses a single personality at every stage.

In the *bori,* she begins as herself, then is *transformed* into the spirit. While herself, she is a mere dancer without rehearsed thoughts, emotions, and movements for the period of her expected possession. It may be argued that there is physiological imitation, since the *mai bori* is costumed in clothing reminiscent of the *iska*: but costume is neutral until it is appropriately invested in the dual personality of *one consciously representing another*, an impersonator-cum-character, an interpreter-interpretation. Since the *mai bori* impersonates no one at any time, the costume she wears acquires not a dramatic value, but a sympathetic-magic value, aimed at attracting the presence of the *iska*.

As soon as the *mai bori* is transformed, she *unconsciously* exhibits 'the demeanour of the spirit' in her dance, and 'her movements, voice, words, knowledge and power will be those of the *iska* "riding" her' (Adelugba,

p. 190). In the *orukoro*, the performer remains an undisguised priest or priestess, performing his/her usual ceremonial duty (offering a sacrifice, for example), communicating with spectators as man with man, until *transformed* into a god or goddess.

As themselves, the *bori* and *orukoro* performers do not, at the same time, assume the behaviour of the spirit, god, or goddess. Conversely, once transformed into the spirit, god, or goddess, they completely lose their own personalities and communicate with spectators as god to man. Writing about 'magical drama', by which he refers to such ritual performances as the *bori* and the *orukoro*, J. C. de Graft states that

> what distinguishes magical drama from all other forms of drama that derive from it is the element of possession in magical drama, the trance state *for which the impersonator in all the derivative forms of drama substitutes conscious intellectual and emotional control during the act of impersonation.* [The impersonator strikes] a fine balance between his awareness of the fictional world of the character impersonated and his awareness of the workaday world of his audience and his artistic self; he knows that no matter how deeply he immerses himself in the role of the functional character there is always a psychological point of safety beyond which he dare not go, lest he be swept out of his depth and get carried away on the uncertain currents of hysteria and ecstasy. In simple theatrical terms this means that the actor loses control of himself (p. 16).

Of course, possession also occurs in non-'magical drama', but it is imitated possession, in which the actor, like the impersonator described by de Graft, has a dual personality. In the work of Antonin Artaud and of Jean-Louis Barrault, for example, 'although actors are required to be 'completely possessed', and the stage directions may specify that whoever plays Panurge 'goes into a positive ecstasy', the effect of spontaneity and anarchistic frenzy was always created from conscious and disciplined rehearsal' (Innes, p. 107). And, in performance, the actor remains himself, 'conscious and disciplined', while at the same time impersonating one 'completely possessed'. This is not the case with the *bori* and the *orukoro*.

Ritual-Masquerade: the 'Owu'

The *owu* masquerade performance (also of the Kalabari) has grown less ritualistic than the *bori* and the *orukoro*. In it, the physiology of the *owu* ('water people', actually water gods), is represented in 'many cloths' sewn together, possibly suggesting scales, and in decorated 'wooden head-dresses' (Horton, 'The Gods as Guests', p. 97.) This interest in appropriate physiological imitation probably arose in the nineteenth century when the *owu* ritual performance became remarkably deritualized. Horton informs us that in some of the *owu* masquerades,

> recreation seems to have broken loose from religion. The motives of dancers and audience in drum-answering competitions are no longer focused on concern for the gods; even less so were the motives of nineteenth-century *Owome* chiefs who combed the Eastern Delta for new plays to devastate their rivals. True, most of the performances involved are preceded by prayer and offerings to the gods represented. But in some cases these seem to have become little more than precautionary measures to ensure that no accidents mar the play. . . . There is little doubt that a secular dramatic form was beginning to emerge from the religious practice (p. 101).

The *owu* engage in three broad kinds of performance: character-sketching dance, re-enactment of a historical episode, and the playing of 'a game of risk'. An example of the first kind centres on Igbo, who falters 'in the serious business of dancing. [He] rushes off for a lecherous advance upon some pretty girl in the audience.' This depicts the major character trait of the *owu* being represented by Igbo – 'a lascivious good-time "bluffer" who can never resist using up all the family funds buying the favours of a woman when his father sends him up-river to buy yams' (p. 99).

An example of a historical event re-enacted is the conflict between Agiri and Sabo. The conflict arises from the attempt of Sabo to prevent the marriage of his sister, Data, to Agiri, whom he considers to have a ruthless nature (p. 99). The 'game of risk' involves the masker and the young men of the village. In a performance at Bile, for example, 'the masker alternately slashes with a matchet [sic] and hurls heavy staves in long, well-directed volleys' at the young men, 'the supply being kept up to him by a retinue of attendants carrying bundles of these staves'. The young men 'compete in creeping as close to the menacing figure as possible' and escaping harm. The game is intended to portray the water people as powerful and ruthless (p. 100).

The artistry in the entire sequence is underlined by the fact that, since the *owu* are gods, not ancestors, their re-enacted lives, character traits, and encounters are fictitious. The maskers creatively imitate and interpret the imagined roles of the gods. They are, at the same time, engaged in a competition, and therefore consciously strive for virtuosity – for not only is bad performance a disgrace to the masker's lineage, but virtuosity is 'one of the most admired achievements in the [Kalabari] community' (p. 98).

Clear-eyed skill is necessary to achieve virtuosity. Hence the incidence of possession is much lower in the performances just described than in the *owu* divination rites (not examined here), which are similar in nature to the *bori* and the *orukoro*. It can even be claimed that what seems like possession in the *owu* masquerade performances – for example, the masker's frenetic and dangerous attack on the young men in the 'game of risk' – is nothing more than intense impersonation, the emotional and intellectual engrossment of the performer in his role, which enables the *owu* masker to exhibit what Horton calls 'possession behaviour' (p. 107) while retaining control of himself.

If at any point actual possession occurred, impersonation would have ceased, and the masker would been have transformed from a performer to a medium. Even then, that transition would have been from impersonation to possession and not from ordinary dancing to possession or from normal personality to mediumship, as in the *bori* or the *orukoro*. However, no clairvoyance occurs in the 'game of risk', which rules out the objective of mediumship.

Thus, the *owu* maskers in the performance sequence just described are impersonators, maintaining dual personalities, imitating the physiologies of 'powerful and ruthless' gods through their costume – which is so elaborate that Horton describes it as a 'burden' which the masker slowly 'vanishes' into (p. 97); their sociologies, through the re-enactment of their interpersonal relationships; and their psychologies, through the representation of their drives and temperaments.

Apparently, there is a sense in which the nature, aesthetic function, and context of a performance may be indicative of the possible occurrence of impersonation. For example, the *bori* and *orukoro* lack impersonation because they are essentially ritualistic – the former being 'primarily concerned with the healing and prevention of illness, but also more generally with [foretelling] good and bad luck' (Horn, p. 186); the latter being 'essentially a performance of worship' which also leads to prophesying 'with the voice of the god or goddess' (Adelugba, p. 209, 211).

Contrarily, the *owu* is essentially more aesthetic than ritualistic, its immediate context being that of 'game', 'play', and 'competition', its essential function to entertain and edify the community, though it still contributes to the community's social and material well-being by attracting the presence of thier gods through representing them, for the seasonal re-inforcement of the covenant between the gods and the community. Thus, while communication in the *bori* and *orukoro* is from god to man, in the *owu* it is between man and man, even though the performance also generates the potential for a man-god communication through other more sacred channels. The ritualistic function of the performance, therefore, derives from its aesthetic nature.

Festival: the 'Osu' and the 'Ogun'

Though a number of ritual performances, such as the *owu*, are events in the African festival, many of them, for example, the *bori* and the *orukoro*, may be scheduled outside the festival at the discretion of the cult or society that 'owns' them. Most traditional African festivals take place once a year. Some performances in them are occult, their methods gruesome, and seeing these may be harmful to the uninitiated. For instance, a non-initiate who sees the rites of an *Ekpo* masquerader of the Efik/Ibibio at night is sure to be pursued and slaughtered (see Enekwe, p. 63). Although such performances have some theatrical content, they are not theatrical in intent, and therefore are not our concern here.

Two public festival performances in which masks are not worn are the *Osu* and the *Ogun*. The *Osu* performance takes place in the *Osu* festival of the Owu/Ijebu of Nigeria. It is an imitation of the capture of Olusen by Iganmigan, a dead tribal hero. This hero is imitated by Chief Asipa, while advancing in dance to pay homage to the king, seated at one end of the arena:

As the Asipa dances on, he makes penetrating moves at the audience, butting in and withdrawing hastily as in a military encounter. . . . It is by far the most tense of the dances, thus showing the fierceness of the battle. When the music changes again . . . there is the relaxed feeling of success (Ogunba, 1978, p. 14).

Olusen, Iganmigan's enemy, who later becomes his captive, is not bodily represented, except vaguely by the audience. And Chief Asipa is not costumed and made-up to look like Iganmigan.

The *Ogun* of Ondo is similar to the *Osu* in some respects. The action imitated is the battle between Ogun, the war god, and an unnamed enemy. However, neither Ogun nor his enemy is represented by an individual: dancers in a procession represent Ogun, while the spectators represent Ogun's enemy. As the dancers move along the route, they make 'dashing, mock-attacks at the audience with their swords, the latter receding good-humouredly and then coming forward again as the "attacker" withdraws' (Ogunba, 1978, p. 21). Again, the dancers do not imitate Ogun's physiology. They are a guild of hunters, to whom Ogun is patron-god; on ceremonial occasions, they turn out in the guild's usual ceremonial dress.

The *Osu* and the *Ogun* both contain a conflict which is not developed in a realistic manner. Yet in neither is the protagonist confronted with a contrarily motivated antagonist. The good-humoured 'receding' and 'coming forward' of the audience, rather than a more realistic simulation of battle between two great warriors, seems to make the battle too easy a ride for the protagonist, and to deny the play the elements of surprise and suspense which would be vital to plotting in the mainstream western theatre.

This is perhaps deliberate; the faith of the community may be weakened by a realistic presentation of their hero suffering the pangs and vicissitude of war, and possibly managing to get off with a narrow escape. Therefore, only the broad outline of the war need be demonstrated, and in a stylized manner. So the conflict develops in waves of music and dance, which gradually increase in intensity and reach a crescendo at the peak of the battle. That a great mass of people here represents a character is an indication of that character's strength, while the momentum of opposing masses indicates the enormity of the battle.

In any case, most members of the audience are familiar with the details of the re-enacted action, and the violent boasts and altercation of the warriors. They are satisfied with a symbolic and formalistic *demonstration* of the battle by individuals, including themselves, dancing as themselves in their own ceremonial dresses, performing their ceremonial duties in real time while sporadically imitating a mythic or historical personage in action. To them, the presentation of two impersonators realistically embroiled in combat is superfluous.

Hence impersonation in both of these performances is mono-dimensional, aimed only at the representation of aspects of the sociology of the hero, particularly his status and relationship with his enemy. The ultimate aim here is not to lead to an understanding of the character, which the imitation of his psychology would bring about, but to rekindle the people's awe of him or sustain their faith in him: for the surest way to demystify a character is to make him understandable. In several respects, therefore, the nature of impersonation in the *Osu* and the *Ogun* is akin to those of performance art: partial, inconsistent, and demonstrative.

Festival Masquerade

Ulli Beier describes a performance of the *Agbegijo*, as played by the Egungun cult of Dahomey:

The masks imitate leopards, monkeys, crocodiles, snakes, tortoises, and other animals. Each animal has to act his part: the monkey scratches; the leopard climbs on the roof of a house and pounces down on a chicken. Often there is a whole scene between a hunter and a leopard. Others imitate people. These may be funny because of abnormal features.... They make fun of ethnic groups: the Hausa man; the Fulani woman; the Dahomey warrior. One of the most amusing masks is usually the European. They [sic] wear masks with long pointed noses, their smooth black hair is made from a Colobus monkey skin. They walk around, stiffly shake hands, and say, 'Howdoyoudo' (p. 224).

Certainly, there is imitation of characters' physiologies in this performance. A headpiece aptly carved, an appropriate animal skin, beak, or horn is used to represent an animal. Each ethnic group or race or calling is represented in its traditional attire and with an item or items usually associated with it, or with a mask depicting the peculiar facial features of its members.

The mannerisms of each group are also imitated: but this cannot pass for an imitation of psychologies, since the characters are not individuated. If, for example, all monkeys scratch, then scratching is insufficient to delineate a particular monkey, let alone show the workings of his mind. And did not all English colonialists on official business 'walk round, stiffly shake hands, and say "Howdoyoudo"'? At best, this reveals a kind of interpersonal relationship, which, like the leopard-chicken and hunter-leopard relationships, comes closer to a sociological than a psychological truth.

Psychological characterization comes more naturally with individuated characters in a developed conflict, which the *Agbegijo*, with its multitude of themes, could not have been designed to achieve. Impersonation in the performance is, therefore, only of generic physiology and generic sociology, making it superficial and light-hearted – intended to generate not awe or sympathy, but laughter.

The same objective and style are patent in a performance of the *Mau* (actually *Mmonwu*) of the Igbo, even though there is an attempt at tri-dimensional impersonation, as here described by G. I. Jones:

A white-faced mask with a cavalry moustache, wearing white ducks and spotless sun-helmet, stalks into the arena and casts a supercilious eye over the scene. The play stops, the mask languidly signals them to proceed, and strolls over to sit among the audience in the seat of honour. This character is Oyibo the White Man (cited in Finnegan, p. 511).

The physiological elements – the 'cavalry moustache... white ducks, and spotless sun-helmet' – evoke the foppery and languid behaviour of a colonial master in the mood for relaxation. The action of the character substantiates this foreshadowing. His signal for the play to proceed is languid because of his low opinion of 'savage' entertainment; he strolls in order not to ruffle his dignity and gorgeousness; he takes 'the seat of honour' without being ushered to it because, among the natives, he claims honour as of right. His pre-eminence and the way he relates to the natives indicate his sociology; his superiority complex, his psychology.

Despite this tri-dimensionality, however, the white man is flat. There is no conflict for him to grow within. Therefore, we cannot know the depth of his psychology. Only his frivolous actions are parodied, as in the *Agbegijo* performance. These contrast with the grave actions which the characters in the *Osu* and the *Ogun* performances are engaged in – actions upon which the continued existence of the performing communities once hung. To the *Osu* performers, Iganmigan is an illustrious ancestor, hero, and saviour; to the *Ogun* performers, Ogun is a god. But the white man, the monkey, and other characters in the *Agbegijo* and *Mmonwu* performances are far less important to their performers. Expectedly, they are treated without awe, solemnity, or depth.

Thus, the value of the character and the nature of his action determine the kind and function of characterization and impersonation. Superficial and caricaturish characterization and impersonation are required in the *Agbegijo* and the *Mmonwu* performances described because of their farcical objectives – if we agree that farce 'aims at producing laughter by exaggerated effects of various kinds and is without psychological depth' and that, in it, 'characterization and wit are less important than a rapid succession of amusing situations' (Boulton, p. 153).

The *Ikaki* of the Ekine society of the Kalabari is our final example of the festival-masquerade. Although, as in many other African masquerades, the myth behind it is not re-enacted, the *Ikaki* re-enacts an imaginative story based on the essence of Ikaki (Tortoise), the central deadly figure in the avoided myth. (Robin Horton, in '*Ikaki*: the Tortoise Masquerade', p. 481–2, relates the myth, which is not relevant to us here.) The *Ikaki* masquerade performance lasts for two days and comprises six scenes. Four of the scenes are enacted on the first day, with a lunch-break after the first two. The fifth and sixth scenes are enacted in the afternoon of the following day.

'Ikaki' in Performance

For convenience, we may identify the scenes as (i) Conflict on the Sea; (ii) Fake Loan Recovery; (iii) Looting; (iv) Arrival of Aboita and Kalagidi; (v) Palm-Tree Climbing; and (vi) Elephant Hunting. An episode of the *Ikaki* story is enacted in each scene, except the fourth, which is mainly one of dance and mime. There are four major performers and they represent Ikaki (Tortoise), Nimite Poku (his 'know-all' son), Nimiaa Poku (his 'know-nothing' son), Kalagidi (his favourite son), and Aboita (his flirtatious wife, actually played by a man). The minor characters, such as the children of the dead king, those with whom Aboita flirts, and those who revive Kalagidi (knocked out in error by Ikaki), are played by members of the audience.

Constraints of space forbid my quoting Horton's description of the performance, which fills nine pages of his book. But its highlights will unfold as we examine the nature of impersonation in the performance If we begin, as usual, with the physiological elements, we note that, of the five major players, only Aboita's physical appearance is not explicitly described, but is suggested by the adjectives 'silly' and 'flirtatious' repeatedly attributed to her:

Ikaki himself, though fairly simply dressed, is readily recognizable by his hunchback and by the schematized tortoise body which is his headpiece. . . . Nimite Poku [is] dressed mainly in a soiled blue-and-white sheet topped with an old felt hat. . . . Nimiaa Poku [is] dressed if anything more shabbily than his brother (p. 483–4).

Ikaki is also suffering from 'elephantiasis of the scrotum – a disease usually regarded as a mark of an evil life', his 'enormous testicles' being represented by a 'wooden slit-gong' (p. 490). Like Ikaki, each of the other major players wears an appropriate head-piece constructed by specialist members of the Ekine society. These physiological elements disguise the players and clearly distinguish one character from another.

The plot is long enough to depict the characters' sociologies and psychologies as well as whether each is round or flat. At every stage of the performance, a particular emotional attitude towards a character is evoked in the audience. We are anxious for Ikaki and Nimite Poku in the first scene, when Ikaki's boat almost capsizes through the negative action of Nimiaa Poku; we laugh Ikaki to scorn when, in the second scene, he is unable to swindle money from the audience by claiming, falsely, that their recently deceased father owed him a large sum; we dislike him for tricking his fellow animals and looting their food supplies in the third scene – and so on. At the climax of the story, in the fifth scene of palm-tree climbing, these earlier emotional hints are distilled into an enduring impression:

But whilst Ikaki is at the top of the tree, blissfully praising himself and extolling the virtues of the palm-fruits . . . Nimiaa Poku has got hold of an axe, and is amusing himself by trying to cut the tree down. Aboita, silly as ever, is flirting with the Ekine people, and so doesn't see what her son is up to. Kalagidi makes one or two attempts to stop Nimiaa Poku but without effect. At last Ikaki looks down and sees what is happening. With an alarmed shriek, he throws his palm-cutting

Performance	Kind of Performance	Kind of Impersonation	Approximate equivalent in western theatre
Bori of Hausa	Ritual	None	None
Orukoro of Kalabari	Ritual	None	None
Owu of Kalabari	Ritual-masquerade	Three-dimensional, realistic-cum-formalistic	Realistic-cum-formalistic
Osu of Owu/Ijebu	Festival	Mono-dimensional and demonstrative	Performance art
Ogun of Ondo	Festival	Mono-dimensional and demonstrative	Performance art
Agbegijo of Dahomey	Festival-masquerade	Two-dimensional, superficial, caricaturish	Farce
Mmonwu of Igbo	Festival-masquerade	Three-dimensional, superficial, caricaturish	Farce
Ikaki of Kalabari	Festival-masquerade	Three-dimensional, realistic-cum-formalistic	Realistic-cum-formalistic

Kinds of impersonation in examples of African ritual and festival performances.

instrument at Nimiaa Poku. But it misses Nimiaa Poku and knocks out his beloved Kalagidi. Ikaki is beside himself. He says he will never come down again. He will hang himself in the tree. [He wails in song for his favourite son.] While Ikaki wails at the top of the tree, Nimiaa Poku rejoices at his escape and dances happily about below. The feckless Aboita...joins him in the dance. Ikaki looks down, sees both his son and wife rejoicing in the midst of his misfortune, and redoubles his threat to hang himself ('Ikaki', p. 489).

Despite our earlier emotions of scorn and dislike for Ikaki, we can hardly fail to empathize with him here. His motivation for climbing the palm tree is to exhibit positive character traits, which we could have sworn he did not possess. Not only does he show that he can perform the feat of climbing the tree, but also that he now works for his own food and wine in contrast to his earlier habit of swindling or looting other people's possessions. He has grown as a character. Our empathy derives (i) from our understanding that Nimiaa Poku, having, in the first scene, attempted to drown Ikaki, Nimite Poku, and himself, deserves punishment for his latest attempt at patricide; (ii) our noting that Ikaki throws his cutting instrument at his son in a moment of utter horror and without premeditation; and (iii) our realization at this point that the theme of the play is that repentance of evil ways and doing good thereafter are no guarantee of a life without pain.

Perhaps our examination of the *Ikaki* already begins to suggest the hermeneutics of classical drama, complete with its plot of a certain magnitude, arousal and eventual purgation of fear and pity, clear and full delineation of major characters, definite structure of conflict development, and resolution – in the last scene, Ikaki kills an elephant to celebrate his family's escape from calamity. Also present in the performance are such features of realistic drama as the largely naturalistic settings (for example, the actual sea is the setting of the first scene, and Ikaki climbs a real palm tree in the fifth); a high degree of individualized characterization and psychological depth; and the retention by each major performer of a particular role throughout the play.

Yet the frequent participation of the audience; the dialogue between the drums and Ikaki in the second scene; the dance and mime in real time which constitute the fourth scene; the contrivance of an elephant with a banana tree in the sixth; the animal characters; the masks worn; and the avoidance of details even in the largely naturalistic settings: all these elements negate realism. The result of this mix is a partly psychological and partly formalistic drama.

Impersonation in *Ikaki* is, therefore, three-dimensional as in classical and in realistic drama. It is more deeply psychological than in the *Mmonwu*, but, as in traditional African folk-tale performance, it is employed and dropped at appropriate times in order to create an illusion and then destroy it before the audience can slip into indolent empathy and deny the performers their much-desired collaboration and criticism.

Conclusion

In all, our findings may be tabulated as on the previous page. But the example of the *owu* masquerade points to the danger of making final statements on forms of traditional African performance, all of which continue to evolve. If we used impersonation as the criterion for drama, we would eliminate the *bori* and the *orukoro*. But that would also eliminate processions,[4] an integral part of the African festival performance, which now feature commonly in written African plays. (It would also eliminate a considerable part of western performance art.)

Perhaps the crucial disqualifier of the *bori*, *orukoro*, and other similar African traditional performances is the entrancement or possession of the performer beyond physical, emotional, and mental self-control. The performances in which this does not occur may be drama of the kinds shown in the table. Though many of them are a part of a festival and may contribute to its religious or ritualistic objectives, the microcosmic context of each within the festival is that of relaxation, in the same way as the dramatic festivals of Ancient Greece took place in a special artistic context within the overall ritualistic context of the City Dionysia. Hence the African festival itself is a partly religious and partly social affair.

It should be stressed that, in relating the traditional performances I have discussed to approximate western theatre forms, I am not trying to 'legitimize' the former by means of the latter. Performance art, which emerged in the western theatre in the 1960s, for example, could scarcely be used to legitimize the *Osu* and *Ogun* festival performances which have existed for several centuries. I have suggested approximate western theatre equivalents simply in the hope that acquaintance with them may aid readers better to understand the nature and function of impersonation in the related African performance modes.

As can be seen from the table, the more realistic the ritual or festival performance, the more intense and comprehensive the impersonation it employs. The performances in which mono-dimensional impersonation occur are largely surrealistic, as more goes on in the subconscious of the performer and the audience than is consciously manifested; those in which two-dimensional impersonation occurs are largely farcical; while those with three-dimensional impersonation may be farcical or serious in a realistic-formalistic way, depending on the depth of psychological representation.

Notes

1. See, for example, J. P. Clark's *Ozidi* (Ibadan: Oxford University Press, 1967); Efua Sutherland's *The Marriage of Anansewa* (London: Longman, 1975); Sam Ukala's *Akpakaland* in *Five Plays: ANA/British Council 1989 Prize Winners* (Ibadan: Heinemann, 1990); and Femi Osofisan, *Morountodun*, in *Morountodun and Other Plays* (Ibadan: Longman, 1982).

2. The following articles, among others, testify to this search: Biodun Jeyifo, 'Literary Drama and the Search for a Popular Theatre in Nigeria', and Demas Nwoko, 'Search for a New African Theatre', in Yemi Ogunbiyi, ed., *Drama and Theatre in Nigeria* (Lagos: Nigeria Magazine, 1981); and Sam Ukala, '"Folkism": Towards a National Aesthetic Principle in Nigerian Dramaturgy', *New Theatre Quarterly*, XII, No. 47 (August 1996).

3. The *mande* dance of Zimbabwe, for example, was considered to be witchcraft by the Southern Rhodesian

colonial regime, and banned by the Witchcraft Suppression Act of 1899.

4. Compare Ola Rotimi's use of imitation as a criterion for drama in 'The Drama in African Ritual Display', in Yemi Ogunbiyi, ed., *Drama and Theatre in Nigeria*, op. cit.

References

Adedeji, J. A., 'Oral Tradition and Contemporary Theatre in Nigeria', *Research in African Literatures*, II, No. 2 (Fall 1971).

Adelugba, Dapo, 'Trance and Theatre: the Nigerian Experience', in Yemi Ogunbiyi, ed., *Drama and Theatre in Nigeria: a Critical Source Book* (Lagos: Nigeria Magazine, 1981).

Albright, H. D., W. P. Halstead, and L. Mitchell, *Principles of Theatre Art*, second ed. (Boston: Houghton Mifflin Company, 1968).

Beier, Ulli, 'Yoruba Theatre', in *Introduction to African Literature* (London: Longman, 1967).

Boulton, Marjorie, *The Anatomy of Drama* (London: Routledge, 1960).

De Graft, J. C., 'Roots in African Drama and Theatre', *African Literature Today*, VIII (1976).

Egri, Lajos, *The Art of Dramatic Writing* (New York: Simon and Schuster, 1960).

Enekwe, O. O., *Igbo Masks: the Oneness of Ritual and Theatre* (Lagos: Nigeria Magazine, 1987).

Finnegan, Ruth, *Oral Literature in Africa* (Nairobi: Oxford University Press, 1970).

Horn, Andrew, 'Ritual Drama and the Theatrical: the Case of *Bori* Spirit Mediumship', in *Drama and Theatre in Nigeria*, op. cit.

Horton, Robin, '*Ikaki*: the Tortoise Masquerade', in *Drama and Theatre in Nigeria*, op. cit.

Horton, Robin. 'The Gods as Guests: an Aspect of Kalabari Religious Life', in *Drama and Theatre in Nigeria*, op. cit.

Innes, Christopher, *Avant Garde Theatre 1892–1992* (London; New York: Routledge, 1993).

Mehta, Xerxes, 'Performance Art: Problems of Description and Evaluation', *Journal of Dramatic Theory and Criticism*, V, No. 1 (Fall 1990).

Ogunba, Oyin, 'Traditional African Festival Drama', in Oyin Ogunba and Abiola Irele, ed., *Theatre in Africa* (Ibadan: Ibadan University Press, 1978).

Ogunba, Oyin, 'Traditional Content of the Plays of Wole Soyinka', *African Literature Today*, IV (1970).

Okpewo, I., *Myth in Africa* (Cambridge: Cambridge University Press, 1983).

Schechner, R., *Performance Theory* (New York: Routledge, 1988).

Stanislavski, Konstantin, trans. David Magarshack, *Stanislavski and the Art of the Stage* (London: Faber and Faber, 1967).

International Congress, Dortmund, 22–25 June 2000

to be held in association with
The German Society for Contemporary Theatre and Drama in English

Broadway on the Ruhr

Current Developments in the Musical Comedy: Production, Management, Performance, and Music Education

The congress will be the first international and interdisciplinary congress in Germany devoted to such diverse issues. As particularly the Ruhr area has developed into a new home for musical comedy, Dortmund is a very appropriate choice as location for our congress. Specialists from the areas of British and American Literature and/or Cultural Studies, musicology, music education, teachers and students of English and music, experts from the fields of composition, theatre and performance studies, the theatre, musical management, town-planning, etc., are invited to join a truly interdisciplinary discourse on current developments in musical comedy.

In addition to papers a substantial amount of practical work in the field – i.e. workshops, practical presentations, performances of musical comedies – will be included in the congress.

Further proposals for papers/workshops/presentations are welcome and should be sent together with an abstract of about 250 words and a short biographical sketch to:

Prof. Dr. Christiane Bimberg, Congress Director, Universität Dortmund, Institut für Anglistik und Amerikanistik, Fakultät 15, Emil-Figge-Str. 50, D–44221 Dortmund

Tel. +49 (0) 231-755-2908   Fax +49 (0) 231-755-5450   E-mail: bimberg@mail.fb15.uni-dortmund.de

Denise Varney and Rachel Fensham

More-and-Less-Than: Liveness, Video Recording, and the Future of Performance

With the spread of digital and other modes of electronic recordings into the auditoria and lecture theatres where performance is studied, the debate about the video documentation of performance – already well rehearsed and in the pages of NTQ – is about to intensify. Rachel Fensham and Denise Varney have based the article which follows on their own work in videoing live theatre pieces for research into feminist performance. This article deliberates on their experience with the medium and examines the anxieties that surface at the point of implosion between live and mediatized performance. The first part locates these anxieties in the question of presence and absence in performance – especially that of the performer, whose body and self are both at stake in the recorded image. In the second part, the authors offer a description of viewing practices, which they present as a model of 'videocy'. Rachel Fensham is Senior Lecturer in the Centre for Drama and Theatre Studies, Monash University, and Denise Varney is Lecturer in the School of Studies in Creative Arts, Victorian College of the Arts, University of Melbourne.

REFLECTING on the state of performance at the close of the twentieth-century show, in which actor/audience relations have collapsed and reconfigured, we might still say of the reified theatre that the audience performs an act of worship before the god of presence, the performance. And through the performance the author, the dramatist, the director, the great actor, and the state theatre are reincarnated. Derrida was right to call this stage a theological space – a space where performance serves the author-creator, and the spectator is mute: 'The theological stage comports a passive, seated public, a public of spectators, of consumers, of "enjoyers".'[1]

Not surprisingly, there are no well-aimed tomatoes, no chattering, no interjections, and no noisy demands for refunds. Seated in the velvet pews of the state theatres, the spectator worships silently, individually, respectfully. By way of contrast, the video recording of live performance is perceived as an entirely different matter – a threat to the sanctity of the live exchange between the stage/altar and the auditorium. Video is a highly portable artefact bringing movies to small domestic spaces littered with food, teenagers' trainers, cans of drink, and home-delivered pizzas.

In large educational institutions, video documentaries are enlarged onto cold white screens in lecture theatres where students watch, catcall, take notes, and make noise. If the video is a recording of a live performance, lecturers, with little respect for the performance's integrity, may stop and start, pause and rewind, inviting students to interrogate the images that play and rewind before them. With more than a little justification, video, it is said, flattens out performance and reflects badly on the aesthetics of theatre.

But the position against video is more than a complaint about poor reproduction standards and the dis-orderliness of spectatorship. Live performance and video are clearly two different modes of viewing, but they are often compared in terms which render video a threat to that essential 'ontology of performance', to use Peggy Phelan's phrase: its *liveness*. Phelan's influential definition of performance would set it against video and other modes of electronic reproduction: 'To the degree that performance attempts to enter the economy of reproduction it betrays and lessens the promise of its own ontology. Performance's being . . . becomes itself through disappearance.'[2]

But to propose that performance can maintain its separateness from mediatized images is to perpetuate, unrealistically, a binary logic of the live and the recorded, the pure and the contaminated, the original and its encroachment. This binary logic cannot be maintained if we want to research performance. Phelan's research is enabled by the reproduced images she scrutinizes in her work – performance artists fail to disappear in the reproduced, mediatized images that support her discourse. Video is a necessary and unnecessarily maligned aid to research; without it, performance disappears and we lose our history and our capacity to think through performance.

The Binary of Presence and Absence

In 1996 we were invited by writer-director Jenny Kemp to make a videotape of her new work, *The Black Sequin Dress*, which had transferred from its premiere season at the Adelaide Festival of the Arts to the Malthouse Theatre, Melbourne. What began as an artist's request for the academy to record her work for the benefit of both parties (we would use the video for teaching and research, Kemp for publicity and promotion) became a complex series of negotiations involving artists' rights, industrial agreements, and contractual arrangements among an ever-expanding number of players.

Paradoxically, the least contentious issue was copyright: that clearly belonged to the writer–director of the theatre production. Making the video was also relatively straightforward under the supervision of postgraduate student Paul Hosking, who has videoed numerous indoor and outdoor performance events. Rather, the drama began over the determination of the right to show and view the video. Our account of the difficulties in making the video recording of *The Black Sequin Dress* and the negotiations over its use were presented at the National Symposium on Research into the Performing Arts in Melbourne in 1997.[3] The negotiations over the viewing rights drew on industrial agreements and copyright law, as one would expect, but they also opened up a range of theoretical questions about the electronic media's impact on the practice of performance criticism, the fixing of the proper objects of study of university Theatre Studies departments, the nature of the relationship between the recording and live performance, and, finally, the practice of video literacy.

This paper contributes to the ongoing discussion, initiated in *New Theatre Quarterly* by Gay McAuley and Annabelle Melzer, of the issues surrounding video documentation. In doing this, we will draw into the discussion the quite considerable contribution of Philip Auslander, whose writings on the subject of 'liveness' and media on the one hand and the notion of presence in performance on the other, make for a productive new understanding of the 'ontology of performance'. We bring these theorists to the table to discuss our own investigations of video literacy as part of the case for the use of video for performance research. This case is set against the restrictive practices of those practitioners and theorists who would oppose it for the sake of preserving the right of disappearance.

Annabelle Melzer notes that video and other electronic arts have already created 'a revolution in teaching methods and research' which 'also provide a fertile locus for discussions in the theory of art'.[4] But she is also well aware of the opposition to video from practitioners such as Peter Brook. In Brook's view the video is subordinate to the performance, its production at best an aid to the betterment of the live event whose interests it serves. Melzer also revisits orthodox views of the video as documentation: that the video recording of live theatre is a useful form of notation or documentation, where the intention is to enable the study of the how-to of theatre production by practitioners.

This view reflects an increasing acceptance amongst practitioners, such as Brook, of the view that the video can act as an aid to the production of theatre documentation. This is, after all, merely an electronic extension of the Brechtian *Modelbuch*. On this model, the

89

video does not claim to reproduce the theatrical event on the basis of equivalence of aesthetic experience, pleasure, or entertainment. Filmed versions of plays usually fulfil this purpose. The Berliner Ensemble produced a 16mm version of *Mother Courage* with Helene Weigel, in which she reprised her stage role, and other more recent filmed plays have included the version of Peter Weiss's *Marat* directed by Peter Brook with members of the RSC. This was utilized by Patrice Pavis, for instance, as evidence of a relation between film and theatre.[5] In contrast to the live performance and the staged-for-film versions, the video is characterized in terms of a series of lacks – the live presence of the actor, the actor–audience dynamic, the atmosphere of the theatre, the filmic shots of the film – and the absence of pleasure and aesthetic value.

The primacy of the live event over the video is thus derived from several sources, affirming both its mystique and its essential liveness. We see in Brook's construction the endurance of the binary of presence and absence in performance, as it privileges the live event over its reduced, derivative other, the video recording. Philip Auslander has already problematized this binary, and the first part of this paper focuses on the anxieties that surface at this point of 'implosion' between the live and mediatized performance.[6] One anxiety concerns the status of individual memory as the legitimate and dynamic record of the performance. Another concerns the performer whose body and self is at stake in the recorded performance.

Legitimizing the Video Image

Gay McAuley, whose Centre for Performance Studies at the University of Sydney has experimented with a number of different recording techniques – from edited and multiple-image recording using three cameras to digital compression – places the onus on the users of such documents to interpret the information contained in them, mindful that what they see is neither 'theatrical performance or television drama'.[7] In other words, it is important for researchers to define their object of study, the video as 'artefact', and to set out the specificity of their viewing practices.

We need to understand the industry perception that the video is a threat to performers' moral rights. (What is it that is slightly shameful about appearing in the auditorium with cables and cameras? Why do we apologise about video?) And, more productively and affirmatively, we need to understand *how* we watch performance on video. What is a video recording of live performance? What does video generate for performance analysis and criticism? In the second part of this paper, we offer an eight-point description of our viewing practices as a response to McAuley's call for responsible viewing, and as a guide to reading the recording medium.

Our major provocation is for Theatre Studies to consider the video as an artefact in its own right that can be theorized outside the binary system into which it has been placed. We wish to free the video for the plurality of its practices and its capacity to produce meaning. We want to unpick the theatre's investment in presence, which rebounds across writers, directors, performers, and their agents, who seek to protect themselves from video, to argue that it is too late to be coy about electronic modes of representation. The future of performance lies in electronics and conduction.

In the meantime, Theatre Studies in Australia has no national archive in which videos can be located and made accessible to the public. At the Lincoln Center, New York, and the Theatre Museum, London, the study of live performance with video recordings has facilitated research by both academics and theatre professionals, and the commercial release of significant recordings from European and American companies has been marketed to the academy specifically for teaching purposes. The peculiarly Australian experience that drives this essay is one in which performance analysis relies upon memories of the performance event which are sometimes prompted by photographic stills (curiously, not the subject of contention).

Yet the video is a frequently used teaching tool across all art forms in Australia – except theatre. Not only do the state theatres deny public access to video documentation of live performances, but independent and small theatres – many of which incorporate video into their performances and which videotape the live event, as does the Melbourne-based company Not Yet Its Difficult – worry about the dissemination of video recordings. Others, who are more amenable to releasing their work on video, such as the Melbourne Workers Theatre, are restrained by industrial agreements. All these regulations constrain the use of video for performance analysis and delegitimize the act of viewing a video. (We make a distinction here between videos of the live performance, which is our own interest, and those manufactured by companies specifically for promotion purposes, where the company retains its artistic control of the images.)

The Memory of Performance

The history of performance analysis throws some light on the enduring prejudice against the video, as the desecration of memory. In the period before the semiotic study of theatre, the stage spectacle was 'considered too ephemeral a phenomenon for systematic study, [and] had been effectively staked off as the happy hunting ground of reviewers, reminiscing actors, historians, and prescriptive theorists'.[8]

A decade later Eugenio Barba, writing in *The Drama Review*, claimed that 'Film and electronics realize what was unthinkable until this century, performances that can be preserved practically unchanged. And thus they obscure the awareness that the essential dimension of the theatrical performance resists time not by being frozen in a recording but by transforming itself'[9] – through being able to transform itself into the 'individual memories' of the 'individual spectators'. Performance is not fixed in time but is changeable within spectatorial memory and remains therefore ephemeral.

There are two initial problems with this argument. On the one hand, it privileges the ephemeral nature of theatre and memory as somehow true to the form of theatre and, on the other, it relies upon individual memories to carry the truths of theatre through time. Surely the very ephemerality of individual memory should make it suspect as a reliable record for a performance truth?

The most obvious thing to be said is that Barba's emphasis on the ephemeral and transformative potential of performance and on the individual's individual memory positions performance within an elitist and bourgeois cultural sphere of the kind we have also described as theological. The most explicit denunciation of this position comes from Roger Copeland: 'The idea that the theatre's "liveness" is – in itself – a virtue, a source of automatic, unearned moral superiority to film and television, is sheer bourgeois sentimentality.'[10]

The more critical question for performance analysis is the status of memory. We are not opposed to memory or the way in which the memory of performance transforms over time, or the way in which the memory of a performance becomes the source for writing about it. But we do oppose a hierarchy of performance reception where memory is the only fit place for performance to be stored. Whose memories are privileged? Historically, it has been those of bourgeois gentlemen and their musings.

We must remember that memory, unless forgotten, is coded; it cannot be otherwise. What this means in terms of performance analysis is that we rely on the already coded narratives of individual memories (actors, directors, theatre critics, etc.), each of whose narratives retells the performance, historicizing it and representing it as discourse. Moreover, memory tends to be non-specific. It conflates different performers, different nights, different performances of the same play, and different settings in different countries. And it does so in the service of discourses such as theatre history or contemporary performance theory which would situate performance in histories of representation.

For this reason, memory is also highly selective: it tends to reconstruct the historically or politically significant performances. Knowing this, certain performances (and their authors and directors) are presented as historically available for memorializing. So Barba is wrong to privilege memory as a storehouse for performance because it protects it from the representational operations of the electronic media. Memory is representational, selective, and stimulated by the persuasive image. And, in analysis, memory is invested with projections and repressions that distort the very events they purport to recall. As Philip Auslander has said of the use of memory in a court of law, where the stakes are arguably higher than for the theatre, 'human memory is not [a] safe haven from regulation and control'.[11] Performance memory does not produce a purer form of truth.

Why is it that Performance Studies still attaches a greater degree of authenticity to individual accounts of performance and to recovered memories than to video recordings? The rhetorical question refers back to Theatre Studies, with its traditional reliance on biographical narratives, and is carried forward in Performance Studies, through the capacity of performance to authenticate the experience of the individual subject. Barba's individual spectator's individual memory is based on *his* experience of the performance which is necessarily subjective – indeed, many would argue that its uniqueness is its strength.

This is considered to be authentic and productive subjectivity because it leads us directly to the experience of the individual subject. But what this means for performance research is that 'recovered memories' of the live event remain unquestioned. The reconstitution of performance through individual and recovered memory is thus rarely referred to by the researcher and it results in generalizations such as 'Wilson's *Einstein on the Beach*', as if each performance is the selfsame thing, existing autonomously and enduring across time and space without any context. Only the theatre reviewer covering the first night is direct about the situation of their reception and his/her experience of a particular performance.

We are not saying that the video is objective, but that different researchers can see the same record and produce different analyses, of which none is more authoritative than any other. And with the video, one is reminded of the social and historical context of the performance through costumes, hair-styles, and accents, as well as the laughter and noises of the audience. These details are often lost in the subtext of memory.

The Presence of Performance

Perhaps the real concern is the possibility that performance will be fragmented and degraded into codes and literal action, as in the worst performance analysis. This view represents an orthodoxy of contemporary performance – that the video displaces the live event and fixes it, as Barba complained, in time. On this view, the video is considered to be a heavily mediated, impoverished image which suffers from the loss of the multiple foci for the spectator. There is a loss of information about the *mise en scène*. It is more heavily framed and the gaze is constructed through the eye of the camera. The specificity accorded to the video appears as a poverty of representation, compared with the 'richness' attributed to the theatre. This poverty of representation is also attributed to the actor, whose presence on video is said to be frozen in time and 'lifeless'.

The actor persists as the powerful factor in this binary. Where Auslander notes 'the anxiety of critics',[12] video produces a major anxiety on the part of actors and those who wish to protect them, such as directors and industrial and legal bodies. Part of this anxiety is about the nature and the quality of substitution, but the predominant fear is that, without their presence, actors will lose control over their image and its distribution. Control over image is enshrined in debates about artists and their moral rights, but supporting that is a philosophical stance on presence which claims that the live body is the manifestation of self. As an agent of self, this body cannot, therefore, be reproduced without the presence of the actor who animates it.

The primary quality associated with live performance is the presence of the living, speaking actor. The live body is privileged – the voice delivered and received without mediation, the palpable energy of the actor and the simultaneity of actions – over its reproduced other, the image. Theatre's liveness and its ephemerality rest on this notion of performance as pure presence. Yet as the processes of deconstruction have shown, representation, on which the theatre relies, is based on absence rather than presence. As for Derrida, 'Presence, in order to be presence and self-presence, has always already begun to represent itself, has always already been penetrated.'[13]

Except during the period of realism, performance has always foregrounded its representational apparatus. Elinor Fuchs has argued that western representational theatre already has imitative and reproductive relations with the real. The notion of performance as a space of presence denies the mediation of linguistic and other semiotic systems that have already inserted themselves into the *mise en scène*, and which have created distance between the performance and the real. Throughout the twentieth century, video and other forms of visual and reproduced film or photographic texts have also 'intruded' upon the performance text, and this has contributed to the supposed de-authentication or 'absencing' in some sense of the speaking subject and pure presence.[14]

Auslander, in responding to Derrida's position on presence, notes that performance is constituted by difference. This discovery of difference, at what was once the site of origin and presence, is further cause for anxiety. The persistence of the notion of presence in performance is linked to the sense of loss experienced in a secularized society:

Having lost what we suspect is the only valid theatre of communal ritual we either rhapsodize about theatres of other times and places or attempt to ground theatrical activity in versions of presence which bear the stamp of secularism, psychology, or political analysis in the place of religion.[15]

The value placed on presence in performance is a form of nostalgia for participation in the communal ritual. It is crucially also a nostalgia for the wholeness of being. Since Schechner theorized performance as ritual, the notion of a community of celebrants (participants who include the actors and spectators in a relationship of faith/belief engaged in a suspension of disbelief) has been celebrated. And while this model of performance criticizes the separation between actor and spectator in the theological stage, it supplants it with an emphasis on the presence of the spectator as holy witness. This dual emphasis on presence, *communitas* and wholeness, had the added advantage of overcoming the perceived problems with representational theatre. A theatre of presence was to replace the theatre of representation.

The Layers of 'Difference'

The contemporary questioning of presence undoes the origin of – and dissolves – the theological stage and the ritual of the event. The writer is no longer the point of origin for the dramatic text, the actor a point of origin for the performance, nor the spectator the point of origin for memory. Indeed, the body and the voice of the actor have always represented presence rather than appearing as unmediated pure presence. This capacity to represent, to appear live, is grounded in the disappearance of the actor's self, and the difference between the actor and his or her self. Even the actor's body alone on the stage does not guarantee presence. As Auslander argues: 'Pure self-exposure is no more possible on a physical level than on a verbal level because of the mediation of difference.'[16] There are always several layers of difference between the actor and truth or pure presence.

A theory of difference refuses the notion of capture and arrival that actors associate with presence. To understand performance as built on difference is to work with a 'productive non-presence'[17] – that is, the multiplicities that flourish once the originary moment (the text, the body, or the self) is set aside. The play of difference in performance shifts authority and authenticity from the presence of the speaking subject to the networks of signification that circulate around stage and auditorium. The actor is no longer the centrepiece of the performance, the 'sign *par excellence*',[18] but, like meaning, is produced by the performance. From the perspective of contemporary deconstruction, the divisions between actor and self, actor and spectator, performance and not-performance are multiple, ambivalent, and dynamic, and occur within the play of differences that constitute performance.

If performance is not constituted by the presence of the actor, but by the actor's several differences from other actors, from his or her own self, from the spectator and so on, then we can no longer claim that performance's essence is its liveness. This is not to say that live performance cannot be said to exist, but that performance is *more-and-less-than* purely present. Theatre is more-and-less-than the *mise en scène* of the theological stage. The before and after of the performance, from rehearsal to critical analysis, are part of 'the play of difference' that makes performance multiple, ambiguous, and dynamic.

The Concept of Videocy

Performance Studies has reified the period between curtain up and down 'as if' it represents the whole: that is, the closure of performance signification. That period, as we know, is also the bourgeois face of theatre that conceals the negotiations and struggles of its production. To be so precious about this public, theological space that the videotape appears to diminish its presence is an affectation that is finally a denial of the obvious point that the actor's presence has 'always already been penetrated'. This more-and-less-than of performance also operates for the actor's presentness in the role and may vary from night to night and stage to stage. Presentness is the trace of the actor's difference in the performance of the role. This prospect is understandably disturbing for performers and their policing agents, and begins to explain their opposition to the video recording and its analysis.

But what is the video recording of the performance? One answer is that the video is a check on the memory of performance. As Erika Fische-Lichte writes, the video is

an artefact [that] allows the recipient to attribute ever new meanings to its various elements, to their combinations and to the structure as a whole; and, whatever the meanings may be, it is possible for others to check them by direct reference to the artefact.[19]

But the video is more than the artefact: it is the agency which mediates a difference between presence and absence, and it does so on several levels. Video can never replace the performance because the one precedes the other. Deconstruction cannot exist without the word, independent of that which it deconstructs. The video retains the traces of the performance just as the performance retains traces of the written text, which itself is the trace of other texts and so on. But the video is not constituted only by the traces of the performance; it maps the viewing of the performance through the eye of the cameraperson and by extension through the eyes of the searchers or researchers. The video is not simply a document or a replacement text either written or performative, and in this sense it is not an agent: it has agency.

This agency is what Gregory Ulmer calls the relay of 'mystory' in which the video structures articulations at three levels of invention: the personal, the popular, and the expert. For the spectator/researcher operating at the expert or disciplinary level, what is needed is 'videocy', or a theory of video viewing. Where Theatre Studies has well-developed methodologies for analyzing live performance, viewing and reading video requires its own articulated approach.

Ulmer adopts a deconstructive process for reading television, the relay of mystory, and asks: 'What are the consequences of difference at the more elaborated levels of discourse and logic?'[20] His work provides a theory for reading the video, in so far as he recognizes that logic (*logos*) is connected with words, and that we need more than logic to deal with video. He asks how we should conduct ourselves in the age of television. Electronically, he says, by reasoning through conduction. 'Reasoning by conduction involves, then, the flow of energy through a circuit.'[21] Ulmer draws on electrical metaphors to posit a mode of reasoning that moves with the images transmitted through the video. Research then becomes a live and energetic circuit of exchange between the video and the viewing and reasoning subjects.

Our use of the *Black Sequin Dress* video enabled us to theorize our own spectatorship, which was active, discursive, visceral, and somatic. As we watched, we were talking, often in a highly animated fashion, and analyzing away from the constraints on the audience in the bourgeois theatre. Our talking was recorded onto cassette tapes, put through a transcription machine, typed into a word-processor, printed for further discussion. The mediation does not stop but it can be made more articulate. We and the performance were plugged into the machinery of reproduction and representation – the tape deck, the recording machine, the computer, the printer, and so on. We were subjects within a circuit of conduction.

Systematizing the Semiotics of Watching

Our experience of using the video recording to analyze performance leads us to a new sense of the signifying capacity of performance. We discovered the following semiotizing processes as specific to this medium.

1 The replay facility of the VCR allows for the repetition of the same as difference. Each time you look at the image in motion something different appears; there is a zoom effect in the looking.

2 The freeze frame. This hold is that which is absent in time: the image becomes like the photograph with a 'punctum' revealing the detail that has and has not been selected; dramaturgical decisions can be examined.

3 The pixellation of the relayed material creates an animation of the surface. The luminosity of skin, shadows, texture, and surface with all its hypnotic effects is apparent. The body of the actor is very much alive and the *mise en scène* is retransmitted.

4 The closeness of the viewer to the screen is highly charged and erotic. The illusion of, and desire for, intimacy with the actor is activated.

5 Surfing between scenes and intensities allows the viewer to read against the grain of the performance. The cutting up of the performance and the redistribution of moments of intensity interrupts the movement of performance text towards the cathartic moment. Critically this enables a researcher to deconstruct the myths which structure the *mise en scène*.

6 The provocation of loud animated responses – viewers can interrupt vocally as much as they like and then interrogate the reasons for those energetic exclamations.

7 The performance is reactivated by the pushing of the stop and play buttons. The perverse (cruel but pleasurable) separation of viewer and video, video and performance, is asserted and intensified through the command of the stop–play.

8 A demand for further urgency and investigation – the immediacy of the exchange activates a desire to look again and again and to theorize the provocation of a particular performance.

This watching process also foregrounds our own formation as researchers. Videocy calls up elements of our daily lives, emotional memories, our personal experience, critical reading, political struggles, etc. Videocy is more-and-less than viewing and semiotizing. Just as all members of the creative team bring many elements to the rehearsal process, so the researchers bring many elements to the post-performance stage of the continuum. Their semiosis rehearses ideas – tries out and discards text – and produces a form of commentary which is like and unlike the recorded event, the performance. The commentary-making is itself alive and energized. The performance and its agents once again make for a very crowded space. There is the reappearance of the chattering spectators.

Critically and emphatically, we do not move out of the space of performance. We still have the reach of the actor, the *mise en scène* and the actor performing for a live audience. The researchers still have to ask, 'What does the performance want to say?' But this is not in order to authenticate any one subject's memory or construction of a live event. Performance is not, as McHoul and Lucy have said of film, just 'a proxy for (or expression of) some person's wants or desires or intentions'.[22] Rather, the video, like performance, is 'an object' able to produce meanings. Both have signifying capacity.

The writing of the researchers is alive to the representations of the performance. The writer/director Jenny Kemp responded with great interest to our video-reading of her play.[23] 'I loved your reading particularly of the physical text of which one rarely gets a reading. . . . Good to be reminded of the power of the physical reading, that it equals or even at times surpasses or overwhelms the verbal text.'[24] Reading returns to the condition of performance as ultimately a circuit of conduction.

We argue that the relation between the video recording of live performance ought not to be an 'either/or' but a 'more-and-less-than' situation. We agree with McAuley that 'the theatrical event always escapes the recording medium',[25] and yet there is a need to develop reading skills – 'videocy' – that do not reduce performance to a network of semiotic systems. The video is like a tentacle of the performance – attached to the performance, but also reaching out for its own destination, pulsating and sucking into new points of connection. Its new spectators plug into its processes of conduction.

Rather than killing off or replacing live performance, as in the 'either/or' model, the video may fulfil an additional task, protecting theatre from redundancy. Discourses about the technologies of performance may ensure that performance is included in contemporary cultural discourse. Without that inclusion, performance may remain sacred, but it will also become increasingly absent from critical theory. As we move into the digital matrix of documentation and analysis,[26] performance cannot remain enclosed in a reactionary metaphysics of presence.

Critical thinking about *différance* – its implications for the notion of the presence of the actor and the deconstruction of the theological stage – occurs as new technologies invade the theatre. Together, theory and technology advance with some urgency – a powerful case for rethinking the ontology of performance.

Notes and References

1. Jacques Derrida, trans. A Bass, *Writing and Difference* (London: Routledge, 1978), p. 235.
2. Peggy Phelan, *Unmarked: the Politics of Performance* (London: Routledge, 1993), p. 146.
3. Rachel Fensham and Denise Varney, 'Documenting and Disseminating Performing Arts Research', in Alison Richards and Angela O'Brien, eds., *Proceedings of the National Symposium on Research in the Performing Arts* (Melbourne: School of Studies in Creative Arts, 1998).
4. Annabelle Melzer, ' "Best Betrayal": the Documentation of Performance on Video and Film, Part 1', *New Theatre Quarterly*, XI, No. 42 (May 1995), p. 150.
5. Patrice Pavis, 'From Theatre to Film: Selecting a Methodology for Analysis. On *Marat/Sade* by P. Weiss and P. Brook', in Jacqueline Martin and Willmar Sauter, eds., *Understanding Theatre: Performance Analysis in Theory and Practice* (Almqvist and Wiksell, 1995).
6. Phillip Auslander, 'Liveness: Performance and the Anxiety of Simulation', in Elin Diamond, ed., *Performance and Cultural Politics* (London: Routledge, 1996), p. 203.
7. Gay McAuley, 'The Visual Documentation of Theatrical Performance', *New Theatre Quarterly*, X, No. 38 (May 1994), p. 192.
8. Keir Elam, *The Semiotics of Theatre and Drama* (London: Methuen, 1980), p. 5.
9. Eugenio Barba, trans. R. Fowler, 'Four Spectators', *The Drama Review* XXXIV, No. 1 (Spring 1990), p. 96.
10. Roger Copeland, 'The Presence of Mediation', *The Drama Review*, XXXIV, No. 4 (Winter 1990), p. 42.
11. Philip Auslander, 'Legally Live: Performance in/of the Law', *The Drama Review*, XLI, No. 2 (Summer, 1997), p. 16.
12. Auslander, 1996, op. cit., p. 203.
13. Derrida, op. cit., p. 249.
14. Elinor Fuchs, *The Death of Character: Perspectives on Theatre after Modernism* (Bloomington; Indianapolis: Indianapolis University Press, 1996), p. 72.
15. Philip Auslander, 'Just Be Your Self', in Philip Zarrilli, ed., *Action (Re) Considered* (London: Routledge, 1995), p. 66.
16. Philip Auslander, *From Acting to Performance* (London: Routledge, 1997), p. 36.
17. Ibid., p. 28.
18. Martin Esslin, *The Field of Drama* (London: Methuen, 1988), p. 56.
19. Erika Fische-Lichte, 'Performance Art and Ritual: Bodies in Performance', in *Theatre Research International*, XXII, No. 1 (Spring 1997), p. 22–37.
20. Gregory Ulmer, *Teletheory: Grammatology in the Age of Video* (London: Routledge, 1989), p. 63.
21. Ibid.
22. Alec McHoul and Lucy Niall, 'That Film, This Paper – Its Body', *Southern Review*, XXVII, No. 3 (1994), p. 303–22.
23. Rachel Fensham and Denise Varney, ' "Help Me, I'm Drowning!" Calls the Man in Jenny Kemp's *The Black Sequin Dress*: Heterosexual Masculinity in Feminist Performance', *Australian Drama Studies*, No. 34 (April 1999).
24. Kemp, letter to authors, 29 April 1999.
25. McAuley, op. cit., p. 183.
26. See Steve Dixon, 'Digits, Discourse, and Documentation: Performance Research and Hypermedia', *The Drama Review*, XLIII, No. 1 (Spring 1999).

Frances Babbage

The Past in the Present?
A Response to Stan's Cafe's Revival of 'The Carrier Frequency'

The premiere of *The Carrier Frequency* took place in 1984, the result of a collaboration between Leeds-based Impact Theatre Cooperative and the novelist Russell Hoban. Impact was founded in 1978 by Claire MacDonald, Pete Brooks, Steve Schill, Graeme Miller, Tyrone Huggins, and Richard Hawley, with Nikki Johnson and Heather Ackroyd joining in subsequent years. Many companies since have cited Impact as a major inspiration, with *The Carrier Frequency* in particular achieving almost mythic status. Today, Impact has long since disbanded, and little documentation of their work remains to enable their legacy to be passed on. In April 1999, the theatre company Stan's Cafe (none of whom had seen the original show) decided to restage *The Carrier Frequency* as part of Birmingham's 'Towards the Millennium' festival; in association with this project, a symposium was held on the subject of 'Archaeology, Repertory, and Theatre Inheritance'. What follows is a personal response to the experience of attending the symposium and performance, and records a variety of attitudes towards myth-making, re-creation, and the potential and problems of documentation. Frances Babbage lectures in Theatre Studies at the University of Leeds.

ON 1 MAY 1999 I attended 'Archaeology, Repertory, and Theatre Inheritance', a symposium organised by Stan's Cafe and held at the Birmingham Repertory Theatre. The papers and discussion focused on issues relating to Stan's Cafe's revival of *The Carrier Frequency* (originally created in 1984 by Impact Theatre Co-operative, in collaboration with novelist Russell Hoban). What follows is less a report than a response, both to the symposium and to the production itself, which I saw on the same evening.

The Symposium

1 I Didn't See It
I didn't see *The Carrier Frequency* in 1984. I never saw any of Impact Theatre Co-operative's shows. The first time I heard of the production was reading Alison Oddey's *Devising Theatre*, trawling it for any references to documentation of devised work, which I was teaching at the time. There weren't all that many (references), but mention was made of the video of *The Carrier Frequency*; working from such a partial record, which for Oddey fails to capture the original show's feeling of excitement and danger, how can she, as a lecturer, communicate her own sense of the show's importance to her students?

The few sentences of description and a photograph from the production somehow lodged themselves in my memory, so firmly that on opening an issue of *Live Art Magazine* and reading that Stan's Cafe were to attempt a restaging of it, I was filled with excitement, heard myself telling my own students how important a project this was, how significant the show to the mid-eighties.

2 The Event(s)
But I didn't see it. I haven't seen the video, any of the (three? four?) versions we learned are in existence. I don't think I've even heard it being discussed before this afternoon, at the symposium organized by Stan's Cafe, and in the evening before and after the performance itself. The symposium – chaired by Andrea Phillips – was deliberately kept as a

small affair, but it was well supported. The Board Room at Birmingham Rep was packed with people wishing to participate in the mythology of Impact in general and of *The Carrier Frequency* in particular.

In the first part of the afternoon the presentations from Barry Smith and Mike Pearson were more general, discussing respectively 'Documentation and Archive' and 'Theatre Archaeology'. After all the talk and a tea break, the focus turned directly upon Impact and *The Carrier Frequency*. Nikki Cooper (née Johnson, a former member of Impact) shared her personal memories of and thoughts about Impact as a company; James Yarker (director of Stan's Cafe) spoke about 'Reviving *The Carrier Frequency*'; Andrew Quick considered 'The Impact Inheritance'. More discussion, a closing, and a three-hour break for those of us intending to see the show that evening at Birmingham's Crescent Theatre.

3 Mythologies

I didn't see it, but I'm interested in mythologies – I wanted to understand this one, maybe feel a part of it. I don't know what everyone else wanted from the afternoon. Maybe to revive the ritual through the myth; maybe to re-vision the myth for a new time, fifteen years on; maybe even to explode it. Perhaps *The Carrier Frequency* was a bizarre, post-nuclear vision of pain and survival. Perhaps it was – as Nikki Cooper suggested, half-seriously – just a group of twenty-somethings thrashing about in water to a loud sound-track. Perhaps both – I would guess it was both. But I don't know; don't ask me, I didn't see it.

4 We Didn't See It

I didn't see it. Nor, bizarrely, did almost anyone else at the symposium. Of the fifty or so people there, one had performed in it and just two had seen it. Some had encountered it *via* grainy pirate video copies. Some had been taught 'The Impact Legacy' at university, in some cases by lecturers who themselves had experienced little or nothing of their work at first hand. Chinese whispers? What is the authority of these words?

5 The Performers, Blind

I didn't see it; nor, in fact, did anyone from Stan's Cafe. James Yarker told us that in their search for performers the company specified that applicants should not have seen the original production. The task the company set themselves was to restage the production, working from the video. The making process lasted two weeks: the first week marking through the video, the second week rehearsal.

Problems and challenges inevitably arose. For instance, gaps in the video-eye perspective had to be filled in by the company. Another dilemma: was that moment, that stumble I saw, a mistake? If so, should my performance edit this out, or should I repeat it anyway? (We were told a story of how Laurie Anderson memorized an audiotaped Japanese version of her own performance text, a translation which had been prepared for her by a native speaker; Anderson had wanted to be able, on tour in Japan, to speak in her audience's first language. The result went down well, although the spectators were surprised she spoke Japanese with a stutter. . . .) Creativity, recreativity.

6 Fragments (unreliably transcribed)

James Yarker: 'We have tried to be true to the video, being aware at the same time that the video may not be true to the show.'

Nikki Cooper: 'I wasn't in Impact with my brain. It was purely emotional. We would have laughed at the idea that what we were doing would ever be discussed, like this, academically.'

Barry Smith: (recalling Beckett's characters, obsessively going over and trying to make sense of the traces of their pasts) 'Something wrong there. . . . '

James Yarker: 'I'm grateful for the chance to play around in someone else's performance.'

Mike Pearson: 'These are not acts of reconstruction, but of recontextualization. They stand *for* the past, *in* the present.'

Unidentified Speaker: 'Do we need to document visual theatre? Maybe it should be passed on simply as rumour, and virus. . . . '

Stan's Cafe's Impact's 'The Carrier Frequency'
A world of water. Scaffolding towers with raised platforms. In the water a table, draped with thick white cloth. A rope strung across the space. Electric lights. Three men, three women. (Six ghosts.) Shades of grey. The men in pale shirts, dark trousers: work wear, for a strange work. Patterned dresses for the women, leggings, heavy manes of hair.

Enter the flood, accept it, walk through it, ankle-deep. Feel the energy required, simply moving in this environment. Scoop water in the hands, pour it onto the white cloth: libations at an altar. Spread the water, smooth the cloth over the table, stroke it, wipe the water off. Take more water: pour it on, spread, smooth, stroke, wipe off. Repeat. Repeat. Repeat. Repeat.

While they do that below, we'll talk. Climb the tower; come up here where it's safe. Sit together, crouch low, rock back and forth.

– *I moan, I moan, odear odear I moan.*
– *Why moan? Noma moan – finkfink strongya.*
– *Okay. Noma moan. Finkfink Erny Warling.*
– *Erny Warling dead. Gone. Thought Nukwa save us. But Nukwa gone too, now. O, I moan.*

Scoop up water. Pour it on the table. Spread it over the cloth, wash it. Quicker. Water on, spread, wash, wipe. You don't have all the time in the world. Repeat, repeat, repeat.

She can't keep going – too weary, too wounded. She's falling – quick, catch her. Carry her through the water, she can't stand. Look, another one dying – catch her, carry her. Now I feel myself falling, floating face down in the water like a corpse. Hands reach for me, arms pull me to the surface, I gasp in lungfuls of air, I am slung over someone's shoulder, carried and stood upright. I am saved – and I run back, throw up my arms and fall again, drowning again. Rescued again, carried again. Repeat, repeat, repeat.

He talks, she falls, he rescues. He falls, she rescues. She talks. Pour, spread, wash, wipe off. Try to leave: run, fight, climb, fall, fail. I moan, I moan.

There is a beauty in this anguish.

Three women, three men. The ritual does not end. Six performers (six ghosts) enter a flooded space, show a world and a way of living. They leave the space but the world remains.

Afterwards

I am grateful for the experience of this production. My description tells, though, not just of what I saw but of what I imagine – my dreaming response to the show, my fantasy. In watching Stan's Cafe I felt I saw traces of an event, not the event itself. If I had known nothing of the project's history, hadn't attended the symposium, my experience would be different. If I had seen Impact's original production, it would have been different again. But I didn't see it. And of course, I still haven't.

NTQ Book Reviews
edited by Maggie Gale

Gail Marshall
Actresses on the Victorian Stage: Feminine Performance and the Galatea Myth
Cambridge: Cambridge University Press, 1998.
£35.00.
ISBN 0-521-62016-3.

Gail Marshall's tightly written study establishes how for much of the nineteenth century the 'serious' Victorian actress was defined – both privately and professionally – by the way in which playwrights, theatre managers and audiences positioned her within the confines of a sculptural metaphor that was authorised and determined by the Ovidian myth of Pygmalion and Galatea. This sculptural metaphor afforded the Victorians a way of achieving an ideal of woman immured in marble and denied access to language, and hence the possibility of articulating independent subjectivity.

Not until the latter part of the century, with the advent of the 'New Drama' (most notably Ibsen) and the emergence of a body of autobiographical writing by actresses in which they spoke and consequently acted for themselves, did the situation change. In the work of Robins and Duse, for example, the male spectator found himself no longer confronted by the attractively draped charms of a doll-like Galatea but subject to the dangerous, revelatory, and emasculating gaze of a petrifying Medusa.

The signifying capacities of Galatea thus permit Marshall to embark upon a subtle re-examination of the familiar distinction of the period between the art of the French actress and its association with (for example) Rachel and Sarah Bernhardt with calculation and immorality, and the apparently artless charm of the English performer, whose 'womanly sensibility' both reconciled the spectator to a reassuring sense of the propriety of the stage and harnessed the sexuality of the English actress's effectively cloaked and simultaneously revealed body to a desirable conservatism.

Marshall pursues her argument with the aid of a variety of sources. These include the 'Living Pictures' of the music hall and the poses of Emma Hamilton as well as manifestations of the sculptural metaphor on the legitimate stage; the representation of the actress and acting in a number of novels (*The Tragic Muse*, *Miss Bretherton*, *Trilby* – and particularly *Daniel Deronda*, which is given a searching reading in the book's pivotal chapter as the 'century's most sustained fictional exploration of the figure of the statuesque actress'); and a number of visual representations, from *Punch* to the classical images of Sir Frederic Leighton and Ellen Terry's first husband G. F. Watts (with Terry's career, both on stage and off, forming a narrative thread throughout the book).

It is perhaps unfortunate that Marshall nowhere breaks the English frame of her study or indicates the resonance of the Pygmalion and Galatea metaphor elsewhere in European theatre during the nineteenth century – for example, at the *fin-de-siècle*, when it would help to clarify the relationship between several major dramatists (including Strindberg, Maeterlinck, and Wedekind) and their actress wives (Harriet Bose, Georgette Leblanc, and Tilly Newes). None the less, one of the achievements of *Actresses on the Victorian Stage* is the framework it establishes for future such research. Marshall's book is finely illustrated, though it assumes a certain familiarity with the theatre of the period and the debates which it has provoked, and to which she now importantly contributes.

MICHAEL ROBINSON

Greg Walker
The Politics of Performance in Early Renaissance Drama
Cambridge: Cambridge University Press, 1998.
245 p.
ISBN 0-521-56331-3.

This is a fine exploration of printed drama in England and Scotland in the period from the accession of Henry VIII to the reign of Elizabeth I. Beginning with some knotty questions well worth asking (Why were these particular plays printed? Why *print* plays at all? For what readership were they printed?) Walker claims that the cultural significance of the printed plays was slight compared with their central importance as performance texts. Arguing against assumptions that great hall drama was conservative, he demonstrates rather that in performance (and as adapted for performance indoors and outdoors) these plays were at the centre of royal and household power and constituted sanctioned spaces for political negotiation and advice.

Individual chapters discuss the plays of John Heywood, Lindsay's *Ane Satyre of the Thrie Estaitis*, Udall's *Respublica*, and *Gorboduc* – providing for each a fascinating new reading, grounded in precise historical research, of the plays' politics.

It is refreshing to see these plays discussed with due attention paid to the *difference* (so often ignored in work on Tudor drama) between plays as performance and as printed objects.

An appendix on censorship shows that there is little evidence of concern to suppress plays in printed form: *performance* was what moved political and religious authorities to acts of censorship or prohibition, and the impact of printed playbooks as potentially 'harmful' literature was minimal by comparison. Another appendix presents a useful bibliography of the 81 surviving plays from the period before 1580, the majority being originally written for performance in a great hall. Admirers of Walker's *Plays of Persuasion* (1991) will seize on this book with delight and much profit.

MAUREEN BELL

Peter Zadek
My Way: eine Autobiographie, 1926–1969
Cologne: Kiepenheuer und Witsch, 1998.
DM 68.00.
ISBN 3-462-02755-0.

Doyen of the *enfants terribles* of German theatre since the 1960s, Peter Zadek was born in 1926 in Berlin and emigrated to England with his parents in 1933. His education was thoroughly English: the progressive King Alfred's School, a period at a prep school, then University College School, Hampstead, and finally Oxford. The first part of this first volume of autobiography, with its title in English (Zadek acknowledges in a preface the iconic status of this song and its singer), gives a vivid account of childhood and youth in Berlin and England, the peculiarities and frustrations of the *émigré* existence, and the cultural experiences that marked the author.

The theatrical events of Zadek's adolescence (pantomimes at the Golders Green Hippodrome and elsewhere, Olivier and Valk in Shakespeare, Charles Laughton as Captain Hook) give way to his own early work in what Norman Marshall labelled the 'other theatre', and in more conventional jobs. As well as such forays into the avant-garde as the London premiere of *Les Bonnes*, Zadek's early career also included weekly rep in Swansea – surely a unique credit in the German theatre world of the last four decades?

There are vivid accounts of great personalities at work, including Tyrone Guthrie directing *Henry VIII*, Joan Littlewood in the 1940s, Barrault as Hamlet in Paris, Tynan (who seems to have cold-shouldered him), and Peggy Ramsay. Of particular interest are reflections on the differences between English theatre in the early 1950s – with 'art' a taboo word among professionals in the dominant 'boulevard' mainstream – and the world of subsidized and cultivated experiment the author found when he returned to Germany in 1958. 'English theatre comes from the circus', he reflects, 'German from the university' – but there are times when, confronted with self-indulgent behaviour in the cosseted German theatres, he admits to nostalgia for the discipline and pragmatism of British rep.

Zadek presents himself as open-minded, without a doctrine of theatre beyond a belief in the imagination ('Phantasie'). He describes a rehearsal method that has sometimes been reticent to the point of absurdity – in one case his failure to challenge until the very last moment an actor who refused to speak above a mutter throughout a long rehearsal period. The insistence on a free imagination rather than pursuit of political or cultural dogma brought him into conflict with more politicized theatre workers and audiences during the 1960s: his account of the controversy over his production of *Saved* at the Freie Volksbühne in 1968, supplemented by materials printed in an appendix, is a fascinating document of the heady days of sit-ins, teach-ins, and demos.

This volume will be valued for its insights (often querulous, sometimes generous) into the personalities and institutions Zadek has worked with, for its account of oppression, exile, and return, and for its unique comparisons of life in very different kinds of theatre over more than forty years. Individual plays and their challenges are revisited, work practices and changes in social and political climate are noted, and sexual and emotional ups and downs remarked on with a frankness rare in theatrical memoirs. A translation into English would be very valuable.

RUSSELL JACKSON

Sharon M. Carnicke
Stanislavsky in Focus
Amsterdam: Harwood Academic Publishers, 1998.
ISBN: 90-5755-070-9.

Greater access to archival material since the dissolution of the USSR has led to a re-examination of many theatre practitioners. Harwood's 'Russian Theatre Archive' series has benefited from the new availability of research, and Carnicke's book provides further evidence of this. *Stanislavsky in Focus*, like Benedetti's *Stanislavski and the Actor* (Methuen, 1998), dispels many of the myths about the 'System' that have been generated by English translations of Stanislavsky's handbooks.

The book divides into three sections: Transmission, Translation, Transformation. Much of the opening section is concerned with the Americanization of the System and its development into the Method. The second section outlines the dissemination of Stanislavsky's ideas largely through the teaching of Lee Strasberg. Carnicke also undertakes a detailed examination of the circumstances that surrounded the Elizabeth Hapgood translations, and led to the production of 'a questionable bible'. There are significant differences in the translation of terms such as *zadacha*, 'task', which Hapgood mistranslated as 'objective', and *deistvie*, 'action', which is inconsistently rendered. In clarifying these terms, and re-examining the Method of Physical Actions, Carnicke and Benedetti have elucidated central concepts which affect the application of the System.

The most original insights into Stanislavsky's work occur in the third section of the book, where Carnicke debates the varied possibilities of 'Stanislavsky's lost term', *perezhivanie* – 'experiencing' – and also anchors the System's use of emotion in his interest in Ribot and Eastern yoga traditions, thus dissociating Stanislavsky from ideas of affective memory. There is also a very interesting, although too brief, discussion of the relationship to Symbolist and Formalist concerns.

Stanislavsky in Focus in practice focuses upon the relationship between the Russian innovator and his American exponents, and, having worked as an interpreter for Lee Strasberg and a visiting director from the Moscow Art Theatre in the 1970s, Carnicke is well placed to elucidate this issue. Though Jean Benedetti's *Stanislavski and the Actor* is a better practical handbook for the application of the System, this book is a valuable contribution to the process of re-examination of the Stanislavsky heritage.

KATIE NORMINGTON

David Williams, comp. and ed.,
trans. Eric Prenowitz and David Williams
Collaborative Theatre:
the Théâtre du Soleil Sourcebook
London; York: Routledge, 1999. 258 p. £15.99.
ISBN 0-415-08606-X.

Williams's sensitive compilation is selective rather than extensive. It starts with *1789*, the production that catapulted Mnouchkine's company to world fame in 1970, followed by *L'Age d'Or* (1975), *Richard II* (1981), *L'Indiade* (1987), and the *Atrides* quartet (1990–1992). It thus omits *1793*, *Méphisto*, *La Nuit des Rois* (*Twelfth Night*), and *Henry IV*, which consitute the Soleil's Shakespeare cycle, as well as *Norodom Sihanouk* (1985), which is closely related to *L'Indiade*. *La Ville Parjure* (1994) and *Tartuffe* (1995), which might have made the publication deadline, are absent, although material available on them is included in the admirable, nigh-exhaustive bibliography. Presumably Williams decided upon his exclusions by the works he thought spoke most eloquently for different elements of the Soleil's concerns.

The key is in the word 'sourcebook', which, while not complete, is very rewarding precisely because it brings together (for the first time in English, moreover) some of Mnouchkine's wonderful interviews – particularly the informative, feisty ones of the 1970s – and those of such collaborators as Philippe Caubère, Georges Bigot, and Philippe Hottier (superb actors, all), Hélène Cixous (the feminist writer and scholar whose writing for the Soleil begins with *Norodom*), and Jean-Jacques Lemêtre, without whose inventions, instrumental and compositional, the Théâtre du Soleil's achievements would have been considerably diminished.

In these interviews are to be found pithy discussions of ideas that have defined the Soleil in its thirty-odd years of performance, starting with the central notion of 'collective creation' that made the Soleil a model for so many groups and troupes across the world. Mnouchkine makes no bones about the fact that all collaborators have their unique and special functions, but that her own purpose is to centralize activity, since this is the role, without hierarchy, of a director. Other notions that are fundamental to the Soleil emerge clearly: for example, *état* or state (the driving mood or passion of a character in the successive moments of a performance); *évidence* or self-evidence (a kind of group epiphany as to who or what is most appropriate for a delimited aspect of work); improvisation, engagement (with social reality), the interrelationship between texts, physicality, and representation, and the liberation afforded by the use of masks. What appears rather hazy, still, is the concept of theatricality which follows the Soleil about like a perfume, but seems to be hard to define.

MARIA SHEVTSOVA

Philip Auslander
Liveness: Performance in a Mediatized Culture
London; New York: Routledge, 1999. £12.99.
ISBN 0-415-19690-6.

'What is the status of live performance in a culture dominated by mass media?' is the central question in *Liveness*. And the response: not much. Disputing dominant cultural constructions of a binary opposition between the live and the mediated, Auslander argues that most live forms have become mediatized. He rejects the 'clichés and mystifications' usually used to 'explicate the value of "liveness"' (e.g., 'the magic of live theatre', the 'energy', as well as work on the topic by 'most scholars in theatre or performance studies', and segues into cultural studies of rock music and American legal practice instead.

These explorations are often intellectually suggestive, as in the careful examination of rock culture's production of its own authenticity (through the mutually validating forms of live performance, audio recordings, and videos), and of the legal system's almost curious continuing commitment to the live trial. They are also very carefully researched, if sometimes rather dependent on the work of others (such as popular music scholar Simon Frith), and sometimes rather over-annotated, with long footnotes more the norm than the exception. These tight focuses form both the strengths and the drawbacks of *Liveness*. On the one hand, they are detailed, critically insightful, and may compel readers across a variety of disciplines (performance/theatre studies, cultural studies, sociology, etc.) to make productive inter-disciplinary connections. On the other, they may focus too tightly on their own precise situations and issues, making cross-disciplinary thinking more difficult, if not inaccessible.

Notions of authenticity and the potential relationships of live performance to 'the law' are examined within these rubrics; but ontology and the material body (complete with material signifiers of sex and race, set within class-stratified cultures) are strikingly less fully explored. Theatre, too, is marginalized; although one of the book's epigraphs is by Forced Entertainment, for instance, they are never mentioned again. In principle, I respect the interdisciplinary movements of the book, but further application of Auslander's suggestive conclusions to theatre itself would have been appreciated.

JENNIFER HARVIE

John Whiting,
ed. with an introduction by Ronald Hayman
At Ease in a Bright Red Tie
London: Oberon Books, 1998. £8.99.
ISBN 1-84002-052-0.

The contents of this selection of John Whiting's occasional pieces – lectures, interviews, and reviews – overlap *The Art of the Dramatist* and *John Whiting on Theatre*, both of which, though published in the 1960s, are still quite easy to find secondhand. The historian will be frustrated at the lack of a comprehensive edition, while the curious may find themselves wondering what all the fuss was about when, in the 1950s, Whiting was considered to be one of the most important figures around.

Like Nigel Dennis, and other intellectuals of the period who were drawn to the theatre but were instinctively conservative in their political attitudes, he has not worn well. An aesthetic purist who believed that 'the theatrical has no place in the theatre today', and who expressed his dislike for the 'ornamentation' of Royal Court directing styles because they got in the way of investigative argument, Whiting now seems, despite his admiration for Beckett and Ionesco, to have been unduly negative about how the theatre might develop in the future.

The most potent items here are a lecture on 'The Art of the Dramatist' from 1957, in which Whiting rails against contemporary demands for 'a communal voice' and attacks the fashion for journalistic playwriting, and a strong review of Sartre's *Les Séquestrés d'Altona* which accurately describes the Romanticism at work in many post-war treatments of Nazi Germany. A fascinated fear of totalitarianism dominates Whiting's criticism as it does his plays, leading to a sometimes strident insistence on the importance of the lone writer. 'The cult of the individual', he complains 'is now almost as great a social crime in the West as it is a political crime in the East.' Viewed at a distance of some forty years, Whiting (who died in 1963, aged forty-five) is increasingly revealed as an authentically Cold War writer locked in the political dilemmas of his time.

JOHN STOKES

Rosemary Pountney
Theatre of Shadows: Samuel Beckett's Drama, 1956–1976
Gerrard's Cross: Colin Smythe, 1998. £12.95.
ISBN 0-86140-407-6.

Beckett's work has had a huge impact on theatre in our century. It poses a problem, however, for anyone trying to analyze its effects, since it does not fit easily into the established categories. It cannot be classed simply as 'absurdist' theatre; it is neither 'playwright's theatre' nor 'director's theatre' (though Beckett made a significant contribution in both roles); and recent academic discussion has failed to conclude whether it will fit better into the modernist or the postmodern category.

This is to say no more than that it is original and innovative. How, then, is the student or scholar to explain this originality? Rosemary Pountney, who is herself an actor, approaches the problem by paying as close attention to the creative process as to the finished work. Working through the rich collection of manuscripts at the Reading University archive, with additional research on collections of Beckett's papers held in Dublin and at half-a-dozen American Universities, she demonstrates how the texts go through a process of painstaking refinement (which Beckett referred to as 'vaguening'), in the course of which process he gradually shaped the evocative and resonant phrases which echo so hauntingly through his plays.

This attention to process is directed not only to the activity of the writer but also to that of the director, and leads Pountney to focus more successfully than most critics on the cyclical and linear patterning in the plays, on Beckett's' working methods, and on his stagecraft. She thereby avoids the temptation that besets most Beckett critics to comment on the philosophical origins and purport of his work, which usually results in earnest affirmations of the master's profundity.

The book is not particularly new. It is based on a doctoral thesis completed in 1978, and revised for publication in 1985 – and the 1998 edition is a reprint, not a revised version of the original. But the work is every bit as useful today as it was when first published because of its copious quotation from manuscript sources. Like *The Theatrical Notebooks of Samuel Beckett* series, published by Faber, it provides us with the raw materials we need in order to reconstruct the creative processes of the playwright. Unlike the Faber series, it is available at an affordable price, and so can realistically be recommended to students or actors. It comes with a recommendation from Barry McGovern, describing it as 'the most useful book (on Beckett) for the actor'.

DAVID BRADBY

L. J. Collins
Theatre at War, 1914–1918
London: Macmillan, 1998. £42.50.
ISBN 0-333-68317-X.

Written by an author who combines an active interest in both the theatre and the services, this is a densely detailed book which explores the relationship between theatre, the army, and war. It begins with a chapter on the theatre's reaction to the First World War, with its recruitment drives both on the legitimate and non-legitimate stages, and also details the complex relationship between theatre workers and those who wanted to accuse them of avoiding signing up for the army. In following chapters on 'The Effects of War on Theatrical Production' and 'Performing for Charity', Collins investigates the ways in which theatre became a vital component of the war machinery.

The various army divisions and POW camps were full of rivalry over productions. Similarly, the work of female impersonators was taken very seriously, with some being 'abducted' or 're-recruited' into different units to participate in productions which were so popular that audiences had to be turned away. VAD nurses, working around the clock, did not get involved in productions: the creation of theatrical illusion, entertainment, and comfort was very much in the male domain so far as the army's participants were concerned.

On a professional level, the various theatrical trade journals and weeklies of the day were full of discussions of war entertainments, government attitudes to wartime arts activities, and so on. Collins weaves such discussions into assessments and descriptions of life at the front, provision of entertainment abroad, war plays, and so on. He also embellishes his analysis with accounts of the work of such up-and-coming professional producer–directors as Basil Dean and Lena Ashwell – although his assessment of Lena Ashwell as self-promoting is a little misplaced. Altogether, this is a well researched and interesting book, invaluable to anyone with an interest in politics and the function of theatre, and early twentieth-century theatre in particular.

MAGGIE B. GALE

Ian McCurrach and Barbara Darnley
Special Talents, Special Needs
London; Philadelphia: Kingsley, 1999. £15.95.
ISBN 1-853-02561-5.

Special Talents, Special Needs is a handbook for teachers and facilitators working with people with learning disabilities. Written by Ian McCurrach, Joint Artistic Director of the Strathcona Theatre Company, a professional company of actors with learning disabilities, and Barbara Darnley, actress and workshop leader, it provides detailed session plans for a year's drama course in a further education setting.

The authors state that learning-disabled people 'are capable of aiming high' and 'can do more, not less, than some people with influence in their lives expect'. They seek gently to steer facilitators away from the pitfalls that learning-disabled drama often falls into: for example, where the end-of-year show is often a simplification of a pantomime or a popular success and where the actors have been drilled in their parts. Such versions of *Cinderella* or *Grease* usually result in displaying the disabilities, not the abilities, of the performers.

Instead, the authors describe closely planned sessions, with warnings as to what can go wrong with each exercise and how then to make it work. There are examples of how to develop the work into performance or for video, with clear techniques for devising around the strengths of the participants. Many of the exercises are tried and trusted drama games with slight but sometimes ingenious adaptations, but there is firm emphasis on the development of acting skills, as for any drama students, and appropriate ways to assess skill development are also suggested. Behaviour problems are tackled, and work with people with profound and multiple learning disabilities is also included.

There is little written about theatre work with people with learning disabilities, and this book is very useful within its terms of reference. What is also needed is work to document and analyze the powerful and challenging contributions made to professional theatre by work such as that produced by Strathcona in London, the Shysters in Coventry, Lung Ha's in Scotland, and others of the growing number of such companies in Britain.

ROSE WHYMAN